THE UNIVERSITY OF
ALABAMA
TRIVIA
BOOK

SECOND EDITION

T0007412

THE UNIVERSITY OF
ALABAMA
TRIVIA
BOOK

SECOND EDITION

JESSICA LACHER-FELDMAN

LYONS
PRESS

Essex, Connecticut

An imprint of Globe Pequot, the trade division of
The Rowman & Littlefield Publishing Group, Inc.
4501 Forbes Blvd., Ste. 200
Lanham, MD 20706
www.rowman.com

Distributed by NATIONAL BOOK NETWORK

British Library Cataloguing in Publication Information available

Library of Congress Cataloging-in-Publication Data

Names: Lacher-Feldman, Jessica, author.
Title: The University of Alabama trivia book / Jessica Lacher-Feldman.
Description: Second edition. | Essex, Connecticut : Lyons Press, [2023] |
    Series: College trivia
Identifiers: LCCN 2023015995 (print) | LCCN 2023015996 (ebook) | ISBN
    9781493069194 (paper ; alk. paper) | ISBN 9781493073542 (epub)
Subjects: LCSH: University of Alabama—Miscellanea. | University of
    Alabama—History.
Classification: LCC LD71.8 .L33 2023 (print) | LCC LD71.8 (ebook) | DDC
    378.761/84—dc23/eng/20230405
LC record available at https://lccn.loc.gov/2023015995
LC ebook record available at https://lccn.loc.gov/2023015996

♾™ The paper used in this publication meets the minimum requirements of
American National Standard for Information Sciences—Permanence of Paper
for Printed Library Materials, ANSI/NISO Z39.48-1992.

This book is an unofficial guide to The University of Alabama history and
trivia and is not endorsed by the school.

CONTENTS

PREFACE

The *University of Alabama Trivia Book* contains a ton of information—some of it is frivolous, some of it is serious, but all of it is true!

Through these snippets of information, one can glean a great deal about this beloved institution—the capstone of higher education in Alabama. From its founding in 1831, The University of Alabama has seen a great amount of history. From the burning of the campus by Federal troops in 1865, to that day in June of 1963 when all the world was focused on Foster Auditorium when Vivian Malone and James Hood walked through those doors to register for classes, and the days and years before, between, and after, The University of Alabama has been a center of life for countless people who have studied there, worked there, or have been diehard fans of the beloved Crimson Tide!

The trivia questions and quotations in this book focus on many aspects of life at The University of Alabama. Chapters on student life and traditions, alumni, faculty, administrative leaders, campus, and of course sports will provide the reader with hours of entertainment, providing mind-bending facts on the triumphant, the brilliant, the funny, and the bizarre. Enjoy!

ACKNOWLEDGMENTS

'd like to thank several people for their insight, creativity, suggestions, and support when I undertook this project long ago, while I was still at The University of Alabama. They include—but are not limited to—Thomas Little, Astro, Merrily Harris, Joyce Lamont, Jennifer Mathews, Erika Pribanic-Smith, Joanna Jacobs, Steve Gillis, and everyone at the W. S. Hoole Special Collections Library. Thanks also go to those whose works on The University of Alabama and Tuscaloosa have helped me so much, especially Suzanne Wolfe, Guy Hubbs, Robert Mellown, and the late James Sellers, and to the countless thousands of people whose lives were touched by UA.

I'd also like to thank all of the amazing people in Tuscaloosa, those who have left us, those who remain, and those who I've never met, for making UA and T-Town such an important place in my memory and in my heart, especially the Rothman family, who are always in my heart, and whose generosity, humor, and kindness make my Tuscaloosa memories all the sweeter. I am also thankful for my Rochester community including Tuscaloosa expats, Paige, and the Hall/Johnson family, who have no trouble celebrating game day in the North, complete with an occasional rack of Dreamland ribs, if we're lucky.

I continue to say, emphatically, Roll Tide! And I thank my wonderful and kind husband and fellow Alabama fan for life, Thomas Little, along with our Alabama-born Luna and our crazy blonde bombshell Cosmo for gearing up with me in crimson and houndstooth fleece in frosty Rochester, New York. *Yea, Alabama!*

INTRODUCTION TO THE SECOND EDITION

Though I have been away from Tuscaloosa and The University of Alabama for over a decade, I was thrilled to have the opportunity to revisit this book and to update it for new readers, the UA community, friends, and fans. I will always consider Tuscaloosa my adopted hometown, and will forever be a fan of the Crimson Tide! Traditions in our household remain that connect us with The University of Alabama, including the sporting of "game gear" on Fridays during football season, where crimson, white, gray, and houndstooth clothing are the only things allowed.

When I was asked to revisit this book, I jumped at the chance, because the process was so fun and challenging for me when I took it on all those years ago. I also learned so much about the university while working on the book. Those of us lucky enough to work in academic special collections libraries and archives become steeped with the history of the institution that they work for, and the compiling and writing of a book like this, where we challenge others to learn more about the place that they love, in this case, The University of Alabama, really feels like a gift to me.

Much has changed since the book first appeared in 2007. We have lost friends and colleagues, the University continues to grow and change, new faculty, students, administrators, and others have joined the community, buildings have been renamed and rededicated, and, perhaps most notably, an unprecedented era of college football unfolded, beginning in 2009 with Coach Nick Saban and all that he brought with him to Alabama. This updated edition brings new facts, new stories, and new names to light, and continues to honor and share the nearly two centuries of history of The University of Alabama.

INTRODUCTION

Trivia isn't trivial. The little snippets of information gathered here, along with quotes from some of the best known and even relatively unknown people who have been associated with The University of Alabama, represent a broad cross-section of life at UA: past, present, and future. As a relative newcomer to Alabama, and to The University of Alabama (and yes, a Yankee), I had my work cut out for me. But as an archivist working with materials relating to the history and culture of this fine university, I was primed for such a task. Trivia is even less trivial for me—as I spent hours looking through campus newspapers, yearbooks, manuscript collections, and other published materials, I found out so much more about the University: obscure facts, forgotten lore, and exciting tidbits that will help me make my job more interesting and, in turn, create future programs and exhibits in special collections that will be of interest to the University community and beyond.

This volume is not meant to represent everything there is to know about The University of Alabama, but rather it gives current students, alumni, fans, and anyone else with an interest in UA some insight into the University's history and direction through the questions and quotes presented here.

I hope that you will enjoy looking through this and stumping your friends with obscure facts as much as I enjoyed putting this together and testing anyone who would listen. Roll Tide!

1 STUDENT LIFE AND TRADITIONS

What is *Rammer Jammer*?

The now-defunct University of Alabama humor magazine that was published from the 1920s through the 1960s. *Rammer Jammer* was a popular and creative outlet for student writers and artists, in the style of the *Harvard Lampoon*, a Harvard University student organization and the world's oldest humor magazine, founded in 1876.

What is the "yellow hammer"?

The Alabama state bird. It is said that Alabama adopted the yellowhammer as the state bird because Confederate soldiers fighting in the Civil War often wore feathers of the yellowhammer in their soft felt hats. The bird is more widely known as the *yellow-shafted flicker.*

What policy regarding "Rammer Jammer, Yellow Hammer!" was put in place in 2003?

The athletics department ruled that the Million Dollar Band could not play the cheer during games. The band is now allowed to play the cheer only once, after a victory.

"My dream is to surround myself with happy, intelligent, energetic and creative people; then I can just sit back and watch the work."
—Glenn House Sr.

What temporary setback did the cheer have in 1987 and 1994?

In 1987, the Million Dollar Band was banned from playing the "Rammer Jammer, Yellow Hammer!" cheer by then-athletic director Steve Sloan because of the word *hell* in the cheer. The ban lasted until September of 1989. In 1994, the athletics department again banned the cheer, this time in response to a request by the NCAA to minimize taunting and fighting at football games. In 1999, the cheer was again allowed, and the band was permitted to play the cheer just once (two refrains) after each victory, though that is often exceeded based on the enthusiasm of the crowd and the significance of the victory. The cheer appeared with just the two lines "Rammer Jammer Yellow Hammer, Give 'em hell Alabama!" sometime in the 1960s, and the full chant evolved from the original sometime in the very early 1980s.

What is the name of The University of Alabama fight song?

"Yea, Alabama!" And though the lyrics are football-specific, they are proudly sung well beyond Bryant-Denny Stadium.

Who wrote "Yea, Alabama"?

It was written by a student! Then–UA student and editor of the *Crimson White* Ethelred "Lundy" Sykes as a response to a contest sponsored by *Rammer Jammer* magazine. He won $50—no small sum at the time—during the 1925-26 season.

What did he do with the prize money?

Sykes graciously donated his prize money to pay for a musical arrangement to be written so the Million Dollar Band could play the new fight song.

Do you know the lyrics to "Yea, Alabama"? They haven't changed and reference a team that is no longer a rival. Which one?

The Georgia Tech Yellow Jackets!

Why isn't Auburn, Alabama's in-state rival, mentioned?

The Alabama-Auburn rivalry was in the middle of a forty-year break when "Yea, Alabama!" was written. The two schools stopped playing from 1907 to 1949. It would be unthinkable to not include an Auburn taunt if we wrote the fight song today!

Why remember the Rose Bowl?

Alabama's 1926 victory against the University of Washington was a defining moment that brought Southern football and The University of Alabama to national prominence. And how!

What is the _Corolla?_ When was it first published? Who was its first editor-in-chief?
The University of Alabama's yearbook. 1893. Thomas Atkins Street Jr.

What are the two student-published literary journals at The University of Alabama?
The _Black Warrior Review_ and _Marr's Field Journal._ _BWR_ is the graduate publication, _Marr's_, the undergraduate journal.

Who was the first editor of the _Black Warrior Review?_
Jeannie Thompson, 1974.

What year was _Marr's Field Journal_ founded?
Marr's Field Journal was created in 1989 as a forum for emerging writers and artists. The journal's annual publication showcases exceptional undergraduate poetry, prose, dance, theater, art, and music composition. _MFJ_ takes great pride in promoting creative thought at The University of Alabama.

"I'm tired of hearing all this talk from people who don't understand the process of hard work—like little kids in the back seat asking, 'Are we there yet?' Get where you're going one mile-marker at a time."
—Coach Nick Saban

> "In Alabama, you better be for football or you might as well leave."
> —Coach Paul "Bear" Bryant

What is "Hilaritas"?

A celebration of holiday music performed on campus annually since 1969, proudly sponsored and coordinated by the School of Music.

Who was the first African-American student to become a member of the UA debate team?

Delores Boyd, who went on to practice law and serve as a judge in Alabama.

How else has the Hon. Delores Boyd contributed to Alabama history?

Boyd is a product of Montgomery's transition in the 1960s from a Jim Crow society. Her high school experience with desegregation is profiled in *Freedom's Children: Young Civil Rights Activists Tell Their Own Stories*. She is also the author of *Jim Crow and Me: Stories from My Life as a Civil Rights Lawyer.*

How much did it cost to attend The University of Alabama in the early 1870s?

$130 per semester (term), which included tuition, board, fuel, lights, attendance, and incidentals. What a bargain!

"There will come a day in your life when you must act for others—your family, perhaps your community—and you must be ready. What you have done to reach this milestone today is part of that preparation. So take from all the books you have read, all the lessons you have learned, the certain knowledge that one day, any day, you must be bold, have courage, and walk through a door that leads to opportunity for others."
—Vivian Malone Jones, in her commencement speech to the UA Class of 2000

Who was the first African-American student to be admitted to The University of Alabama?
Autherine Lucy, in 1956.

How was she honored in 2022?
The University of Alabama dedicated Autherine Lucy Hall in honor of its first African-American student, Dr. Autherine Lucy Foster, in February 2022. Previously named for former Alabama governor and Ku Klux Klan leader Bibb Graves, the building was renamed Lucy-Graves Hall by the UA Board of Trustees on February 3, 2022, in a nod to Lucy, without removing Graves's name from the building. The System then, eight days later, named the building solely in honor of Autherine Lucy Foster.

What was the Cotillion Club? Where did these programs take place?

A club that organized dances, balls, and other functions on campus. In the era of the big band, they brought famous dance bands to campus, such as Harry James and His Music Makers, Tommy Dorsey, Les Brown, Benny Goodman, and Spike Jones. Those programs took place at Foster Auditorium.

When was Foster Auditorium built? What kind of a project was the construction?

Foster was built in 1939 as a Works Progress Administration (WPA) project during the Great Depression, and was funded by federal grants. The building has been used for Alabama basketball, women's sports (in the 1970s and 1980s), graduations, lectures, concerts, and other large gatherings, including registration.

Who is Foster Auditorium named for?

It was named for University of Alabama president Richard Clarke Foster. President Foster died in office in 1941.

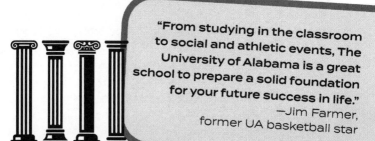

"From studying in the classroom to social and athletic events, The University of Alabama is a great school to prepare a solid foundation for your future success in life."
—Jim Farmer, former UA basketball star

What year were the Blackfriars founded? What did they do?

Founded in 1906, the Blackfriars was a dramatic performance group at The University of Alabama in the early twentieth century. The group was organized by Professor F. D. Losey. The troupe staged professional performances, specializing in Shakespeare, but also commissioned and performed original plays.

Who were the Corolla Beauties?

They were female UA students, who were selected each year to be featured in full-page photographs in the yearbook.

Who chose the Corolla Beauties for 1949?

Billy Rose, legendary Broadway producer and lyricist. Other judges through the years included Rock Hudson, Pat Boone, Jackie Gleason, and UA football hero and Hollywood cowboy Johnny Mack Brown, probably many of them by mail!

How many Greek associations, fraternities, and sororities are recognized on the UA campus today?

The UA Greek community comprises 35 percent of the undergraduate student body and is home to sixty-eight social Greek-letter organizations and over eleven thousand students. Since Fall 2011, The University of Alabama has held the coveted honor of being the largest fraternity and sorority community in the nation with regard to overall fraternity and sorority membership.

Who are the McNair Scholars?

An elite group of students who, as juniors and seniors, work with faculty mentors and conduct research. This national collegiate program is named for Dr. Ronald E. McNair, an astronaut who died in the *Challenger* space shuttle accident in January 1986.

Why were the stairs at what is now known as Reese-Phifer Hall seldom used?

A campus legend said that only women of dubious virtue dared climb the stairs—probably due to the combination of wind and skirts on the massive staircase. This legend persisted until the 1970s when dress codes for women were abandoned.

What was "Mark's Madness"?

UA's student organization of basketball fans named in honor of then-coach Mark Gottfried.

What long-gone local student hangout was known for "good things to eat"?

Pug's cafeteria. The restaurant was a popular breakfast place on homecoming and sometimes used sixty dozen eggs preparing breakfast that day.

What exciting new feature did Pug's offer UA students in the Fall 1955 semester?
Access to their new "TV Room"—which featured a rare color television for students to enjoy. Televisions were rare in general, but a color TV was an oddity and a great attraction!

In one of her regular National Public Radio commentaries, former UA English professor Diane Roberts described walking by an on-campus fraternity house and seeing its front yard occupied by a live goat, and a bathtub containing a sleeping young woman in full evening dress. Which fraternity was it?
The Delta Kappa Epsilon (DKE) House.

When was the first televised pep rally in the history of The University of Alabama?
November 22, 1955, televised on WBIQ Channel 10 in Birmingham and WTIQ Channel 7 on Mount Cheaha (the highest point in the state!).

Who was Alabama playing?
Auburn.

"All I see is that grass and open field, and I just run like there's no tomorrow."
—Former Alabama running back Derrick Henry

> "The University I graduated from has faded into vaguely familiar forms that loom large only in my memory. But I do not lament this fact. I celebrate it. Because the campus that I knew has been replaced by something grander, more impressive, more humane, more inclusive."
> —Gay Talese, 1949 UA graduate, from his 2001 UA Commencement address

In what year did the BAMA Radio Network begin broadcasting?

1942. It evolved into WABP, the first student radio station at UA.

What unlikely pair roomed together at UA in the Spring 1942 semester?

George Wallace and "Shorty" Price.

In 1956, how many date nights were freshman women allowed (!) weekly?

Three: Friday, Saturday, and one other night of their choice.

What was used as a shield in the nineteenth century in a duel to determine the university steward?

According to a 1933 *Alumni News Magazine*, a side of bacon.

> "We're not going to talk about what we're going to accomplish. We're going to talk about how we're going to do it."
> —Coach Nick Saban talking about "his process" during his introductory press conference in 2006

When women were first admitted as students to UA, what did they wear?

According to a letter from the president of the university in 1901, they were required to wear "a simple black uniform consisting of an Oxford cap and gown, in all public places, especially when attending your classes." Yes, basically, a graduation-style cap and gown!

In what year did individual photographs of undergraduate students first appear in the *Corolla*?

1913. Before that time, it was all group portraits.

What senior honor society for men was founded by the Class of 1914 and still continues its practice of tapping new members on the Mound annually on the first Tuesday of May?

The Jasons.

What change did the Jasons undergo in 1976?
They were officially banned from campus by the UA administration for not admitting women.

The Jasons Honor Society, the oldest society on campus, was founded in 1914. In 1933, UA officials allowed the Jasons to use the Little Round House next to Gorgas Library as the organization's home. The structure was converted into a memorial for all honor societies in 1990, but is still known as the "Jasons Shrine."

What group was founded to help remedy this?
There is a women's honor society at UA, the XXXI. The name, roman numerals for the number 31, is a play on the University's founding year, 1831.

Which student made national news in 2000 when she attempted to integrate UA's Greek system?
Melody Twilley. She went on to help found the Alpha Delta Sigma multicultural sorority in 2003.

> "UA's music department attracts a diverse group of students and professors who are knowledgeable in various fields of expertise."
> —Ishbah Cox, then–UA Future Faculty Fellow, 2000

What UA freshman successfully integrated the traditionally white sorority system in 2003?

Carla Ferguson, a freshman from Tuscaloosa. She was offered a bid by Gamma Phi Beta sorority.

What was "Guidon"? Who were among its first members?

A military fraternity for women. A chapter was established at UA in 1935. Margaret Denny, the daughter of then-President Denny, and Mary Harmon Black, the future Mrs. Paul "Bear" Bryant.

What is Get on Board Day?

The annual campus-wide extracurricular activities fair, held on the Quad.

Who was the first Student Government Association (SGA) president? Who was he named for?

Lister Hill, who went on to be a US senator. His father named him for Dr. Joseph Lister, under whom he studied. Dr. Lister was the pioneer of antiseptic surgery and the namesake of Listerine!

"One of the fundamental assumptions of UA has been that education ought to give a man or a woman a place within themselves to stand: a solid platform from which hopes may leap, ambition march, or dreams fly."
—Winton Malcolm Blunt, 1941 UA graduate

> "You guys gave us a lot of really positive rat poison. The rat poison that you usually give us is usually fatal. But the rat poison that you put out there this week was yummy."
> —Coach Nick Saban

When was the SGA officially formed?

The SGA became official in 1914, though its initial formation as an organization for students to govern themselves began in 1907.

What year did the famed UA humor magazine *Rammer Jammer* cease publication? What publication replaced it?

In 1956, after thirty-one years. *Mahout* replaced *Rammer Jammer*.

What is a "mahout"?

A Hindu word meaning the keeper and driver of an elephant. Clever!

Where did the name "Million Dollar Band" come from?

The name "Million Dollar Band" is purported to have been bestowed in 1922 by W. C. "Champ" Pickens, an Alabama alumnus. That name lives on one hundred years later!

Besides pumping up Tide fans and players at games, what did the Million Dollar Band do in January of 1949?

They participated in President Harry Truman's inauguration in Washington, DC.

What are UA's colors? Where did UA's colors come from?

Crimson and White, of course! They were adopted after their use in the 1885 New Orleans Exposition competitive drill by UA's cadet class Company E, which won first place.

What legend is associated with the Denny Chimes?

Passed down by students (of course!), it is said that bricks will fall from the monument on the head of any virgin who walks too close to the chimes.

What prestigious honorary society was first established at UA in November of 1850 in secret?

Phi Beta Kappa.

What was the first student society established at UA with the mission of the "promotion of literature and science"?

The Erosophic Society, in May of 1831, the year the University was founded!

What were the Latin mottos of the Erosophic Society and Philomathic Society, respectively?
The Erosophic Society: *Sapientia Praestat Omnibus* (Wisdom Precedes All).

The Philomathic Society: *Pro Virtute et Patria* (For Valor and Country).

What is Derby Day?
A spring celebration and competition between sororities at UA.

What is "Pomping"?
The act of making elaborate and brightly colored signs with chicken wire and tissue paper for UA's homecoming weekend.

Where are these signs displayed?
On Sorority Row.

What fraternity hosts the popular spring contest that once featured elaborate skits performed by various sororities and even the crowning of a queen of the derby?
Sigma Chi.

"Great pair, says the Bear."
—Advertising slogan for Golden Flake potato chips and Coca-Cola

In October 1941, a dance was held on campus to collect what for GIs?
Cigarettes! Times have certainly (thankfully!) changed.

What happened to the *Crimson White* in 1942?
The editions were made physically smaller because of a wartime effort to conserve paper and a lack of advertising.

What is the oldest women's organization on campus?
The YWCA, which established a branch on campus in 1899.

What was the *Alabama Belle*? What was her fate?
The University of Alabama's replica nineteenth-century showboat. After only a few short months on the water in 1974, she sank in the Black Warrior River, was raised by divers, but then sank again! Not to be confused with the *Bama Belle*, which also provided cruises on the Black Warrior River and was offered for sale in 2020, another casualty of the COVID-19 pandemic.

Who was the first African-American homecoming queen?
Terry Points, who won in 1973.

Who were the "Alabama Cavaliers"?
A college band at UA—and one of the largest in the South. They formed in 1929 and played through the 1950s.

What was the *Bama Beam*?

The University of Alabama's engineering magazine.

What UA student organization founded in 1997 brings a little-known (in America!) sport to T-Town?

The Crimson Cricket Club. The club is made up largely of UA students from India, and is now part of a confederation of teams in American College Cricket, which started in 2009 and is made up of over one hundred clubs from around the United States. The University of Alabama Cricket Club is also involved in community service in and around campus, and helped remove tornado debris and rebuild houses.

What is the Mallet Assembly and where do they live?

A self-governing men's residential honorary, founded in 1961. Counter to its definition, the Mallet Assembly does admit women, and not all Malleteers (as they're called) live in Byrd Hall.

> **"My total experience as a student at this great institution was rewarding and long-lasting. Friendships made there have enriched my life and become more meaningful.**
> —Woodrow W. Clements, former UA student (1933–1935)

What student organization, which celebrated its fiftieth anniversary in 2021, has recorded full-length albums?

The Afro-American Gospel Choir, founded in 1971. The choir also travels throughout the Southeast representing The University of Alabama as a recruitment resource and also representing our diverse communities as a form of outreach.

The soundtrack to which mid-1970s off-Broadway musical was a favorite for the DJs at WVUA during the 1980s?

Tuscaloosa's Calling Me, but I'm Not Going by Hank Beebe, Bill Heyer, and Sam Dann.

FACULTY

Name the historian and UA history professor emeritus who won the prestigious Lincoln Prize in 2003 for his book *Fredericksburg! Fredericksburg!*

Dr. George Rable.

What former UA English professor is known for discovering a previously unknown poem by William Shakespeare?

Dr. Gary Taylor, who discovered the poem "Shall I Die? Shall I Fly?" in 1985 while on the UA faculty.

What former UA professor designed the long-used red, white, and blue crest used as the emblem for Ford vehicles?

Art professor Frank Engle. He taught at UA from 1949 until 1980.

> **"I knew a lot of intellectuals in Tuscaloosa. They just took their football a little more seriously than the ones in Cambridge or New Haven."**
> —John Jerome Cochran, 1963 UA graduate and NBC News correspondent

What nineteenth-century University professor went on to have a college named in his honor? What Northern college is named in his honor?

F. A. P. Barnard, an antebellum UA professor of astronomy. He was the first professor hired for the UA College of Engineering. Barnard College. He taught for many years at Columbia College (now Columbia University). Barnard is a women's college affiliated with Columbia.

What Pulitzer Prize-winning author teaches in the Journalism Department and can tell a story like no other?

Rick Bragg. He is the author of several books, including *The Prince of Frogtown*, *Ava's Man*, and *All Over but the Shoutin'*. He received the 1996 Pulitzer Prize in Feature Writing.

Who left The University of Alabama in 1837 and opened the noted antebellum Greene School for Boys ten years later?

Henry Tutwiler.

What did prize-winning novelist Russell Banks (author of *The Sweet Hereafter* and *Cloudsplitter*) take back home with him after his time as a visiting professor in the UA English department?

A spouse. While in Tuscaloosa in 1987, Banks met Chase Twichell, a professor in the MFA program, and they were married in 1989.

> "When we git up to the University, Coach Bryant he come out to the gym where we all settin' in our shorts and sweatshirts an begin makin a speech. It 'bout the same kind of speech Coach Fellers would make, 'cept even a simpleton like mysef could tell this man mean bidness! His speech short and sweet, an conclude with the statement that the last man on the bus to the practice field will get a ride there not on the bus, but on Coach Bryant's shoe instead. Yessiree. We do not doubt his word, an stack ourselves into like flapjacks."
>
> —The words of Forrest Gump, from *Forrest Gump* by Winston Groom (Doubleday, 1986)

Name the UA history professor who served as the longtime editor of the *Alabama Review* and did extensive research and writing on the Gorgas family, as well as on Sarah Gayle, the mother of Amelia Gayle Gorgas?

Dr. Sarah Woolfolk Wiggins. Dr. Wiggins was also a pioneer as one of the first women to teach in Arts and Sciences.

What retired UA faculty member was awarded the prestigious Carnegie National Outstanding Doctoral and Research Universities Professor of the Year in 2001?

Professor Cornelius Carter, of UA's Department of Theater and Dance, making us all very proud in the national spotlight!

> "High among the duties of a university is the encouragement of intellectual curiosity. I am deeply indebted to UA in this respect because it was there that I developed a love of reading and a curiosity to learn."
> —Robert G. Gillespie, former UA law student

What soon-to-be bestselling author left his job as a professor at UA under a cloud of mystery in 1927?

Carl Carmer, author of *Stars Fell on Alabama*.

What highly regarded and loved professor in the Art Department never completed more than a high school diploma?

Al Sella.

What former UA professor held the Coal Royalty Chair in Poetry at UA in 1990?

George Starbuck.

Two volumes of the poet's work, which were published posthumously, were coedited by a UA professor. Who was it?

Dr. Elizabeth Meese. Dr. Meese specialized in feminist theory. She was a professor in the English Department, which named an award for her, the Elizabeth Meese Memorial Award in Feminist Theory.

Name the beloved UA faculty member who wrote several Alabama history textbooks used in Alabama schools for decades.
Dr. Charles A. Summersell.

Who is the UA faculty member and department chair considered to be one of the foremost experts on the relationship between Thomas Jefferson and Sally Hemings?
Dr. Joshua D. Rothman. His scholarship includes several award-winning books as well as some tasty research on barbecues in the South, and how barbecue has become a cultural phenomenon.

What former UA professor published a book on her great-grandmother, the "official White House hostess" who took over for an ailing first lady?
Elizabeth Tyler Coleman, who taught English at UA, wrote a biography of Priscilla Cooper Tyler, who served as the official White House hostess for her father-in-law, President John Tyler, after his wife suffered a stroke. *Priscilla Cooper Tyler and the American Scene 1816–1889* was published in 1955.

> "With the mellow tones of Denny Chimes in the background I found, through the challenge of outstanding professors . . . that studying and learning are exciting experiences."
> —Frank Minis Johnson Jr.,
> 1943 UA Law School graduate

What UA professor of geology was appointed to be the first state geologist in Alabama?

Professor Michael Tuomey. He was appointed in 1848 and served until his death in 1857.

What "military man" brought the Million Dollar Band into national prominence? Where did the Colonel get his rank?

Colonel Carleton K. Butler, who led the band from 1935 to 1968. The title of Colonel was conferred upon him by the University's ROTC in 1938.

Name the mid-twentieth-century UA faculty member who founded and directed a world-renowned string quartet at UA? What did his students call him?

Professor Ottokar Čadek. Professor Čadek joined the faculty in 1943 and headed violin instruction and chamber music until his death in 1956. His students called him "Papa." He was from a long-established musical family whose members continue to hold prominent positions in the classical music world. On July 25, 1956, Čadek was a member of a quartet performing one of Johannes Brahms's quartets when he collapsed on stage and passed away.

"As long as you know within yourself—and the guys with you know it—that you have confidence in the plan, you know you are not going to fail."
—Coach Paul "Bear" Bryant

> "I can remember vividly the exhilaration walking across the Quadrangle in the late afternoon, the sunlight filtered to a dappled mat spread across the parched grass. A tinge of self-righteousness brought on by this studious expedition made the climb up the library steps seem less steep. Echoing in the still air, the comfortable ring of Denny Chimes gave the day a reassuring sameness."
> —Libby Anderson Cater, UA graduate (1946)

What former UA professor served as a consultant for Steven Spielberg's film *Amistad*?

Dr. Howard Jones. His book *Mutiny on the* Amistad received wide critical acclaim.

Name the author who both graduated from and taught at UA who penned an important work that he did not live to see published.

Clarence Cason, a 1917 UA graduate and author of *Ninety Degrees in the Shade*, an important work about aspects of Alabama history and life. His life ended tragically just days before the book was released.

What former faculty member and UA graduate received the Ordre des Palmes Académiques from the French government in the 1950s?

Professor Wade H. Coleman.

> "Some of the great leaders in history were not adored but respected. My advice to leaders: Stop trying to please everyone and do what you believe is best."
> —Coach Nick Saban

Which famous novelist and short story writer published an essay in the *New Yorker* recalling his experience of being robbed at gunpoint in front of a downtown Tuscaloosa bar during his time as a visiting English professor? Which bar was it?

Andre Dubus, author of *In the Bedroom*. The bar was the famed "Chukker," now long gone, but not forgotten.

Name the former UA professor who gained international notoriety in 1997 by leading a mass suicide. What did he teach?

Leader of the Heaven's Gate cult, Marshall Applewhite, also known as "Do," in reference to the musical notation. Applewhite taught organ at UA in the late 1950s.

What former UA art professor made architectural models of original campus buildings for UA's 125th anniversary in 1956?

Howard Goodson.

Who was the first woman on the UA faculty?

Amelia Gayle Gorgas, who stepped in as University librarian upon the death of her husband, Josiah.

What former UA professor served as president of Sweet Briar College for twenty years? On what Alabama native did she author a biography published by The University of Alabama Press?

Anne Gary Pannell, a strong, resilient, and dedicated educator, and the then-youngest woman ever to earn a doctoral degree at Oxford University. Dr. Pannell wrote the 1961 biography of another fierce educator of women, *Julia S. Tutwiler and Social Progress in Alabama.*

What former UA dean, faculty member, and alum helped organize the Oak Ridge Nuclear Studies Institute?

Dr. Eric Rodgers. He received his bachelor's and master's degrees from UA in 1931 and 1932 and taught in the Physics Department for almost forty years.

"My memory teems with pictures of thousands of students with an amazing variety of careers on campus and after graduation. I taught at least one bishop-to-be, artists, actors, novelists, and so many others that the list would quickly get out of hand. Academic friendship is a tremendously important element in education (I think these days are underrated). The University of Alabama has enriched my life with generations of friends—mentors, fellow students, colleagues, and my own students. I am grateful."
—George Burke Johnston, UA graduate and former UA professor and assistant dean

What campus building is named in his honor?

Eric and Sarah Rodgers Library for Science and Engineering is named for Professor Rodgers and his wife.

What did Sarah Rodgers do at UA?

Professor Sarah Rodgers taught statistics in the College of Commerce and Business Administration for more than forty years. She received her bachelor's degree from UA.

What former UA professor has his works in the permanent collections of over a dozen major museums?

Professor Richard Zoellner. Professor Zoellner taught art at UA from 1945 until 1979, remained active with campus life, and exhibited work until his death in 2003 at the age of ninety-four.

What program did Professor Zoellner create on campus?

Zoellner established one of only two departments of fine art printmaking in the Southeast at UA in 1945.

Which former UA professor was knighted by the King of Sweden? On whom did he write a critically acclaimed biography?

Hudson Strode, professor of creative writing. Strode wrote, among other things, a widely read biography of Jefferson Davis.

> "When I was a kid, Tuscaloosa was on par with the North Pole as a magical destination. Instead of Santa Claus, Tuscaloosa had Bear Bryant. Even the town's name—which derives from the name of an old Choctaw chief—suggested someplace remote and magical."
> —Warren St. John, from *Rammer Jammer Yellow Hammer* (Crown, 2004)

What former UA professor wrote a definitive work on Walter Lippmann and freedom of the press?

Professor John Luskin, who taught at UA from 1938 until 1974.

What former UA professor led an effort in 2005 to produce "Memories: Perspectives of Black History," to document the voices and stories of the people who were involved in the tumultuous days of the struggle for civil rights in Tuscaloosa?

Dr. Jerry Rosenberg, who taught in Psychology and served as the director of UA's New College Radio Lab.

What former faculty member was the winner of the first Kennedy Center-Rockefeller Foundation International Piano Competition in 1978?

Professor Bradford Gowen of UA School of Music. He received a standing ovation following his performance at the Kennedy Center.

> "Sure I'd love to beat Notre Dame, don't get me wrong. But nothing matters more than beating that cow college on the other side of the state!"
> —Coach Paul "Bear" Bryant

What former UA English professor is internationally recognized as an expert on authors and the experience of war?

Dr. Philip Beidler. Dr. Beidler, a beloved professor and friend to many, authored many works and documented his own experiences in military service. He was also the author or editor of several books relating to Alabama authors.

What UA professor established the debate team on campus?

Annabell Dunham Hagood. The team won national championships under her guidance in 1949 and in 1955.

How many instructors were in the nursing college when it was first established at UA?

Just one! The program grew exponentially from there, and moved to Birmingham in 1967. The Capstone College of Nursing at UA opened in 1976, and is recognized as a national innovator in clinical simulation in nursing education, utilizing simulators and telehealth technology in teaching, research, and health care delivery.

What former UA professor is an internationally known scholar of Jacques Derrida, having translated three of his major works?

Dr. Richard Rand. Rand taught in UA's Department of English, and edited two works on this French philosopher.

What former UA professor helped establish two museums relating to African-American heritage in Alabama?

Dr. Amilcar Shabazz.

> "I didn't meet Dr. Denny until I registered for admission to the law school at Alabama. . . . He asked me to walk over to his office with him for a talk. He talked about the law school and about his son, a recent graduate. He suggested that I study my classmates as well as my books, since he expected that school to produce the future leaders of this state. . . . I soon found out that Dr. Denny was right—the leadership which would guide this state was in the law school. The associations formed there have directly influenced my entire life."
> —George LeMaistre, UA Law School graduate (1933)

What former UA professor and alum penned the novels *From Hell to Breakfast*, *Night Fire*, and *The Secret Pilgrim*?

Ed Kimbrough, who received degrees at UA in 1939 and 1940, and taught in the creative writing program from 1941 until his death in 1965.

What former UA professor was the first graduate of UA's radio arts program?

Roy Flynn, who joined the faculty in 1944. Flynn was also a published fiction writer.

What former UA professor recorded more than five hundred songs, including lullabies, African-American gospel and secular songs, temperance songs, and work songs in the 1940s?

Folklorist Byron Arnold, who taught in the Department of Music. His papers are held at the Hoole Special Collections Library and include recordings and transcriptions/lyrics. His 1950 book *Folksongs of Alabama* highlights his research, and a later book, published in 2004, *Alabama Songbook,* was edited by UA professor and dean emeritus Bob Halli.

"In 1915, I left Tuscaloosa, but I never left the University."
—Joseph Lister Hill, UA alum

> "Everybody hits me up for eating Little Debbies, but no one passes that cookie jar."
> —Coach Nick Saban

What former UA history professor contributed to the monumental work, *I'll Take My Stand: The South and the Agrarian Tradition*, published by Harper Brothers in 1930?

Frank Owsley. His essay is entitled "The Irrepressible Conflict."

What former UA professor was one of the most prolific and influential scholars of early America, the Founding Fathers, and federalism, and penned a definitive biography on Alexander Hamilton?

Dr. Forrest McDonald.

What unusual sartorial study habit did Dr. McDonald admit to on a C-SPAN book program that was aired on national television?

When home alone, he prefers to work in the nude.

What UA professor has written and edited extensively on the complex topic of the work *Gone With the Wind*?

Dr. James "Andy" Crank. Dr. Crank is also a recognized expert on a variety of topics relating to American literature and culture, with special focus on Southern literature, Alabama authors, Harper Lee, Randall Kenan, Sam Shepard, drama, film, hip-hop, and queer issues.

> "Undaunted, I attended my first class, escorted not only by guards, marshals and policemen, but also by two female students who eagerly showed me the way to my first class. The picture of this event was printed throughout the world and produced joy on the part of those who wished us success and also caused us to receive hate mail simply because we dared to be friendly towards each other."
> —Vivian Malone Jones, the first African-American UA graduate

What former UA professor and geologist was an early champion of the rich natural resources of Alabama?

Eugene Allen Smith, a naturalist who traveled by mule-drawn wagon throughout Alabama after the Civil War to find natural resources that could be used to develop industry in the state. His efforts in working with the state legislature also resulted in permanent funding for the Geological Survey of Alabama and a building, now the Alabama Museum of Natural History, on The University of Alabama campus designed by Smith to house his collections and the collections donated by others, as well as classrooms and laboratories for students. Smith Hall is, of course, named in his honor.

Name the former UA professor who was a champion of state constitutional reform.

Bailey Thomson, an Alabama native and UA journalism professor, advocated for constitutional reform and for improved conditions for impoverished Alabamians. He was a founder and chairman of Alabama Citizens for Constitutional Reform.

ALUMNI

Who is the only UA alum to date to have won two Pulitzer Prizes?
The internationally known and beloved Dr. E .O. Wilson (BS 1949, MS 1950) won two Pulitzer Prizes, both in the nonfiction category. He won in 1979 for his book *On Human Nature* and in 1991 for his book *The Ants*, and was a *New York Times* bestselling author for *The Social Conquest of Earth*, *Letters to a Young Scientist*, and *The Meaning of Human Existence*.

What UA cheerleader and homecoming queen went on to win two Emmy Awards and a Golden Globe, in addition to penning a *New York Times* bestseller?
Sela Ward (Class of 1977).

What UA alum, known for his comical Southern drawl and his rich baritone singing voice, has a star on the Hollywood Walk of Fame? What character was he best known for?
Jim Nabors (Class of 1952). Gomer Pyle on the *Andy Griffith Show*, and the successful spinoff *Gomer Pyle, USMC*.

In what other area of entertainment has Jim Nabors excelled?

Music! Jim Nabors recorded well over thirty albums of mostly easy listening pop music in his lifetime, earning three gold records.

What far-out psychologist enrolled at The University of Alabama in 1941?

Timothy Leary. He was alleged to have been expelled for spending the night in a women's dormitory, losing his student deferment, and was drafted into military service in 1943. He then took college courses at night and earned a BS from The University of Alabama that same year. He went on to earn a PhD from UC Berkeley, and was a leader in the counterculture movement in the 1960s.

"No one can help but be aware of the rich tradition that is associated with this team and this University. Tradition is a burden in many ways. To have a tradition like ours means that you can't lose your cool; to have tradition like ours means you always have to show class, even when you are not quite up to it; to have tradition like ours means that you have to do some things that you don't want to do and some you even think you can't do, simply because tradition demands it of you. On the other hand, tradition is that which allows us to prevail in ways that we could not otherwise."
—Dr. David Matthews, UA president, 1969–1980

What UA alum sold more books than any other American author between the two world wars?
T. S. Stribling. He even outsold his leading contemporaries, Faulkner and Hemingway, and is considered by many the leader of the Southern Literary Renaissance. Though not widely read today, his work is important and still resonates with readers.

What Tuscaloosa native and UA graduate is considered one of the most important physicists of the twentieth century? What were his three older brothers known for?
Robert Jemison Van de Graff, inventor of the Van de Graff generator. Football! Adrian (Class of 1912), Hargrove (Class of 1914), and William T. "Bully" (Class of 1915) Van de Graff all played for the Crimson Tide.

What 1906 UA Law School grad served on the US Supreme Court?
Hugo L. Black (1886–1971).

What UA alum went on to produce such films as *Die Hard* and *Field of Dreams*?
Charles (Chuck) Gordon, a former ZBT at UA.

Name the two well-known cousins who both are in UA's Communication and Information Sciences (C&IS) Hall of Fame.
Mel Allen and Elmo Ellis. Both men were giants in the world of broadcasting.

What other hallowed halls does Mel Allen grace?

He has been honored by the National Radio Hall of Fame, the National Baseball Hall of Fame, and the Alabama Sports Hall of Fame.

What honors has Elmo Ellis earned? What distinction did Elmo Ellis have while a student at UA?

Too many to list—but among them a 1966 Peabody Award and UA's highest individual accolade, the Hugo Black Award, in 2000. He is the only student to ever serve as editor of three main UA student publications: the *Crimson White*, the *Corolla*, and the now-defunct humor magazine *Rammer Jammer*.

What UA alum and famous composer's nephew went on to invent the teleprompter, revolutionizing live television?

Irving Berlin Kahn, Class of 1939.

What UA alum earned three degrees in seven years?

Mike Stevenson. He began his study at UA in 1994, and by 2001, he had received his bachelor's, master's, and doctoral degrees in metallurgical and materials engineering—at an impressive pace!

What well-known fiction writer graduated from UA in 1949?

Borden Deal, author of several novels, including *Walk through the Valley.*

> "In Tuscaloosa, Alabama, which Western fans didn't know was on the map, is the abiding place of the Pacific Coast Football championship today."
> —The *Los Angeles Evening Herald* after Alabama's stunning defeat of the Washington Huskies 20–19 in the 1926 Rose Bowl

Before penning his first of many novels, what did prize-winning author William Bradford Huie do after graduation from the UA in 1930?

He lived in Tiflis, in the then-Soviet Union, and returned to the United States to lecture and write on Russian life, writing for such magazines as the *National Republic*. Huie went on to write prolifically both as a journalist and novelist.

What two Alabama governors served as SGA presidents?

George Wallace (1942) and Don Siegelman (1967).

What MFA in creative writing graduate has authored several novels and has had one of her works adapted into a film? Where did she find her source material for this work?

Nanci Kincaid. Her 1998 novel, *Balls*, brilliantly captures the experience of living as a coach's wife. She was the spouse of college football coach Dick Tomey.

> "Those of us who were students at the UA in the early sixties were especially fortunate because we were forced to grapple with the moral problem of segregation. . . . So when I left the campus in 1963, I felt very lucky. I had been present for a bit of history. I had known people of grace, dignity, and quiet courage. And it had instilled in me a respect for, and a love of, learning."
> —John Jerome Cochran,
> 1963 UA graduate and NBC News correspondent

What former UA student was a well-known author and astute businessman, as well as a decorated war hero and established art collector?

William March Campbell, who wrote under the name William March. He was a World War I Navy Cross and Croix de Guerre recipient, wrote several novels and short stories, and was a vice president for the Waterman Steamship Company. His final novel, *The Bad Seed*, gained success as a book, a Broadway play, and a film, which sadly he never lived to see.

Who was the first director of the Million Dollar Band?

Dr. Gustav Wittig, who led the band from 1913 to 1917. From 1917 to 1927, it was led by students.

What 1905 UA School of Law graduate was awarded a Pulitzer Prize in Letters in 1933?

T. S. Stribling, for *The Store*. Though not read often today, it was an instant bestseller when *Time* magazine called it "easily the most important US novel of the year."

Which graduate of The University of Alabama College of Communication and veteran of UA's NPR affiliate WUAL became the national host of *Weekend All Things Considered* in 2005?

Debbie Elliott.

What UA alum was *King for a Day* on January 11, 1957?

Dr. R. C. Partlow (1912) was featured via telephone on this popular early television program.

What cum laude graduate of UA went on to serve as the first director of the first state archives in the United States?

Thomas McAdory Owen (1866–1920). He was the founding director of the Alabama Department of Archives and History in Montgomery, which was founded in 1901, making it the oldest state archives in the United States.

What Tony-winning actor and UA alum (MFA, Alabama Shakespeare Festival) has joked that he has "the worst name in show business"?

Norbert Leo Butz. He is a two-time winner of the Tony Award for Best Actor in a Musical, and is one of only nine actors ever to have won the award twice.

Name the UA alum who went on to serve as CEO of Texaco and as a director of the American Petroleum Institute.

John Key McKinley—he holds both a bachelor's and master's degree from UA.

What UA alum got his start on the silver screen with Buster Crabbe?

Yancey Brame, also credited as Bruce Lane and Yancey Lane (AB, 1926; AM, 1928). He appeared in several small film roles in the 1930s and 1940s.

What UA alum wrote a book which was voted "the best novel of the century" as voted by librarians across the United States?

Harper Lee! Her novel *To Kill a Mockingbird* won her a Pulitzer Prize and has been translated into over forty languages. It continues to be a staple in high school English classes across the United States and is beloved by millions.

"All he's ever talked about is how much he loves The University of Alabama. Now that I'm in school there, I understand why."
—Jessica Namath, former UA student and daughter of legendary UA quarterback Joe Namath

What recent literary phenomenon has *To Kill a Mockingbird* also dominated?

The "One Book" program, where an entire community reads the same book. *Mockingbird* has been chosen for this project many, many times because of the important and complex issues around race and family that it addresses.

What honor was Harper Lee given by the Peck family? What literary endeavors did Harper Lee take on as a UA student?

Gregory Peck's grandson is named Harper in her honor. Peck received the best actor Oscar in 1962 for his role as Atticus Finch in the film adaptation of her novel. Ms. Lee was active in literary matters, such as serving as the editor of *Rammer Jammer*, the University's literary and humor magazine, and writing the "Caustic Comment" column for the University newspaper, the *Crimson White*.

What student, who transferred to UA from Transylvania University in 1831, became its first graduate, earning his AB at UA's first commencement in 1832?

John Augustine Nooe.

What UA alum and Tuscaloosa native was a long-term US senator?

Richard Shelby.

What UA alum, former SGA president, and former Shelby chief-of-staff was elected to replace him?
Katie Boyd Britt. Britt is the first woman to be elected to the US Senate from Alabama.

What 1941 alumna served as a member of the Woman's Auxiliary Ferry Squadron and ferried both B-24 and B-26 planes to airfields and ports during World War II?
Nancy Batson, Class of 1941.

On what magazine was she a "cover girl"?
She appeared on the cover of *Air Force Magazine*, complete with her leather bomber jacket and parachute!

What UA alum was responsible for bringing Dr Pepper to the masses, making it more than just a regional drink in Texas?
Woodrow Wilson (Foots) Clements. He was the CEO of Dr Pepper from 1974 to 1980, and was inducted into the Beverage World Hall of Fame in 1982.

What UA alum wrote a play that was turned into a 1958 film starring Anthony Quinn and Shirley Booth?
Lonnie Coleman (1942), whose play *Next of Kin* was made into the film *Hot Spell.*

What UA alum wrote for such television shows as *Laverne and Shirley* and played the role of the "mad scientist" in 1950s Chiquita Banana commercials?

Paul B. Brice, a 1950 UA graduate.

What former senator and congressman (not from Alabama!) graduated from The University of Alabama in 1921?

Senator Claude Pepper. Senator Pepper was active in public service in the state of Florida from 1929 until his death in 1989.

What Class of 1956 graduate and winner of the Frank Thomas Memorial Trophy and the Jim Moore Memorial Trophy went on to do some very big things in a very cold place?

Bart Starr! A former UA quarterback, he became a superstar with the Green Bay Packers and a superstar in life!

What other UA alum also played and coached with the Packers?

Don Hutson, who retired from pro football with four all-time records.

Which UA graduate celebrated her wedding in the President's Mansion?

Lua Galalee Martin, daughter of Dr. Galalee, UA president, 1948–1953.

What UA alum penned mystery novels along with some important historic bibliographic work on Confederate Imprints (material printed in the South during the Civil War) and nineteenth-century maps?

Sara Elizabeth Mason (Class of 1932).

What UA graduate is credited for the discovery of aureomycin, an important antibiotic?

Dr. Benjamin Minge Duggar (Class of 1891).

What UA alum was known for a time as "the statehood senator"?

Hon. Ralph E. Moody, who was selected to the Territorial Senate for the then-Territory of Alaska. He went on to serve as Alaska's attorney general from 1960 to 1962.

What UA alum was best known as the father of the Blue and Gray football game?

Champ Pickens (Class of 1898).

What was Champ Pickens's early role in Alabama football? What was the result of that telegram? What was the score of that game?

It was Champ who sent the telegram to the chair of the Tournament of Roses Committee in 1925 to draw his attention to UA's winning record. Two weeks later, Alabama had a bid to the bowl. Alabama beat Washington 20–19!

What UA alum won the 1976 US Open Championship and returned to UA to complete his degree in 2001?

Golf legend Jerry Pate.

What other member of the Pate family graduated that year?

Jerry Pate's daughter Jennifer received her degree in Human Development and Family Studies the same day!

What UA alum served as the editor of the *Crimson White* while a student in 1963 and facilitated articles that documented the integration of The University of Alabama?

Scott Henry (Hank) Black Jr.

Name the UA alum who helped pen the controversial novel *The Body Politic* with Lynne Cheney, former US vice president Dick Cheney's wife? What other VPs has he been associated with?

Vic Gold, a UA Law School grad. He was the press secretary for Spiro Agnew and a speech writer and advisor for then-vice president George Bush under the Reagan Administration.

> **"I've been thrown out of better places than this."**
> —Shorty Price, UA super fan, as he was being ejected from one of many UA football games

> "So I want everybody to think here for a second. How much does this game mean to you? 'Cause if it means something to you, you can't stand still. You understand? You play fast. You play strong. You go out there and dominate the man you're playing against and you make his ass quit. That's our trademark. That's our M.O. as a team. That's what people know us as."
> —Coach Nick Saban's pregame speech to the team before a 2008 victory at LSU

What former *Crimson White* sports editor had an early start creating the experimental and literary column titled "Sports Gay-zing"? Besides his brilliant journalistic career and several well-known books, what honor was bestowed upon him in 2004?

Gay Talese (Class of 1953). One of his most well-known pieces, "Frank Sinatra Has a Cold," was labeled "The Greatest Story Ever Told" in *Esquire*'s seventieth-anniversary issue—calling it the very best article in *Esquire*'s long history of excellent articles. Not to be outdone, *Vanity Fair* called the piece "the greatest literary-nonfiction story of the 20th century." Definitely worth the read!

What UA alum was a campus leader in the early 1970s and was one of the first presidents of UA's Afro-American Association?

John Bivens.

What UA grad served as attorney general and governor of Alabama, and had a starring role in a 1955 film?

John M. Patterson. The film, *The Phenix City Story*, was a sensational film noir drama about the real-life murder of Patterson's father, the newly elected attorney general Albert Patterson.

What UA alum and former president of the Chicago Medical School was a recipient of a Horatio Alger Award?

Dr. John J. Sheinin. Dr. Sheinin came to Alabama from Russia as a teen with just $4 in his pocket.

Name the former editor of the *New York Times* who received his master's degree from UA in 1973?

Howell Raines.

What former UA alum played football with the Tide and professional baseball, and then after World War II made monumental strides in yet another sport? What was the name of his inspiring book, published in 1969?

Charley Boswell. After losing his sight in World War II, he went on to win twenty-eight US and international blind golf championships and served as an advocate for vision-impaired athletes and as an inspiration to countless others. *Now I See* is the book about his triumphant experiences.

What UA alum was the first African-American Bama Belle and a founding member of UA's Afro-American Association, now called African-American Association?
Diane Kirksey. She was also the first African-American member of the homecoming court.

Whose voice will always be remembered as "the Voice of the Crimson Tide"? Where was he seen weekly?
John Forney, whose play-by-play was heard by countless thousands for years. As co-host of weekly television shows with Alabama head coaches Paul "Bear" Bryant and Gene Stallings.

What UA alum was the first woman to serve on the executive committee of the American Accounting Association?
Dr. Catherine Miles, who received her MS and PhD from UA in the early 1950s.

"I just wanted to thank God for giving me the opportunity to coach at my alma mater and be part of the UA tradition."
—Coach Paul "Bear" Bryant

What UA alum with a ferocious nickname is considered the father of modern amphibious warfare?

General Holland M. "Howling Mad" Smith, USMC, who received his LLB from UA in 1903.

What UA alum, who served as president of one of the largest manufacturing corporations in the world, was once told by a professor that he'd never recommend a man for a business career who spent his time in college "picking a banjo"?

Knox Ide, who graduated from UA in 1923, made his way to New York in 1931 after graduating from Harvard Law School and maintained a successful law career in Anniston. He later served as president of American Home Products Corporation. Let's hope he still picked a banjo in his spare time!

What UA alum wrote award-winning children's books and served as an airplane mechanic in the Women's Army Corps in World War II?

Aileen Kilgore Henderson. Her first book for children, *Summer of the Bonepile Monster*, won the Milkweed Prize for Children's Literature in 1995 and the Alabama Library Association Award in 1996. She was also a fierce advocate for historic preservation in Tuscaloosa.

Who was the first woman to earn a law degree at UA?

Mable Yerby, who later became Mrs. James Lawson, received her LLB from UA in 1920.

What famous Alabama brothers and UA graduates went on to Congress, with one serving in the US Senate and the other serving in the US House of Representatives? Among their other distinctions, what did they each do in turn?

Senator John H. Bankhead II and Congressman William Brockman Bankhead, respectively. Both brothers had a part in raising the internationally known and beloved actress Tallulah Bankhead. After the death of her mother, William's daughter Tallulah was raised by her uncle John and his wife.

Who was the last surviving Confederate soldier who had been a UA student?

John Flournoy Ponder, who passed away in 1943 at the age of 95.

Who was the first African-American executive vice president of the SGA and a student representative to the UA Board of Trustees in 1975?

Sylvester Jones. Sylvester Jones was a leader who blazed new trails for others to walk with him. His gift and passion was the ability to establish friendships across the boundaries of race, religion, and philosophy. The Sylvester Jones Leadership and Career Resource Center at UA is named in his honor and serves the entire UA student body.

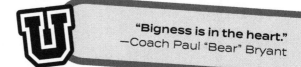

What UA alum has won three Emmy awards and a Peabody? With what two national heroes was he photographed as a student?

John Cochran, who received a BA from UA in 1963. John was well known as a senior correspondent for ABC News and was their top correspondent who covered the White House from the Nixon to Obama Administrations. He was shown in an iconic photograph with President John F. Kennedy and Paul "Bear" Bryant, among others, at the White House. In the photo Cochran can be seen peeking over then–UA President Rose's shoulder.

Who gave John Cochran his first broadcasting job?

Another UA alum Burt Bank, now a fellow UA College of Communication and Information Sciences Hall of Famer. Bank hired Cochran when he was a student to announce records and read the news at WTBC Radio in Tuscaloosa.

What did Burt Bank found in 1953? What horrific event has made Burt Bank's name widely known?

The University of Alabama Football Network. Major Burt Bank was a survivor of the infamous Bataan Death March.

Name the UA alum whose grandfather is credited with inventing the typewriter.

Gordon Sholes, whose great-grandfather Christopher Sholes patented his "type-writer" in 1868 and also developed the now-standard QWERTY keyboard configuration.

What former UA student helped found the CIA? What else was he known for? What legacy did he leave behind?

Miles Copeland Jr. He was an established jazz trumpet player and one of the first white musicians to play with an all-Black orchestra. He played with Erskine Hawkins as well as other bands, most notably the Glenn Miller Orchestra. Besides his diplomatic work and publishing, his three sons, Miles III, Stewart, and Ian, all have had incredibly successful music careers: Stewart was the drummer of the band The Police, Miles was the founder of IRS Records, and Ian was a major concert promoter and booking agent.

> **"The circular structure was to reflect enlightenment, a sign of a modern university, because as the English universities used the church as their focal point, both [The University of Alabama and the University of Virginia] used their libraries, housed in the rotundas, as their focal points, which was a secular view at that time, separating education and religion."**
> —Dr. Robert Mellown, professor of art history, on the Rotunda

> "Have a goal. And to reach that goal, you'd better have a plan. Have a plan that you believe in so strongly you'll never compromise."
> —Coach Paul "Bear" Bryant

Who was the first African-American student to earn a PhD from UA?

Dr. Joffre T. Whisenton, in 1966. He served as the president of Southern University, an HBCU in Baton Rouge, Louisiana, from 1985 to 1989.

What former UA student was crowned Miss Universe in 1967?

Sylvia Louise Hitchcock. As a junior at the University when she won the Miss USA title, Hitchcock chose not to complete her degree. She was a member of Chi Omega sorority.

What internationally recognized artist and photographer received two degrees from UA? Despite decades of living and working in Washington, DC, from where did he draw much of his influence?

William Christenberry, who received a BFA in 1958 and an MA in 1959. Christenberry was from the Alabama Black Belt, and he made frequent trips home to Tuscaloosa and to Hale County, Alabama, during his lifetime. It could be said that the Black Belt of Alabama was his muse.

Which graduate of the Alabama Shakespeare Festival's Professional Actors' Training Program (in cooperation with the UA Department of Theatre and Dance) received the 2001 Emmy for Outstanding Guest Actor in a Drama Series for his portrayal of a demented serial killer on TV's *The Practice*? What was his first and most famous role on the New York stage?

Michael Emerson. He played Oscar Wilde in Moises Kaufman's play *Gross Indecency*. And most people know him immediately as Benjamin Linus on the TV show *Lost*.

According to the October 1943 UA Alumni Magazine, how many living alumni were in military service at that time?

There were approximately six thousand people, or 25 percent of the alumni, in all theaters of war.

What UA alum was the first woman to ever serve as the State Department spokesperson? To what country did she serve as ambassador?

Margaret Tutwiler (1973). She was the ambassador to Morocco.

What UA alum was one of the first African-American graduates of the UA School of Law and was appointed to the UA Board of Trustees in 2004?

Hon. John England. Judge England is a former member of the Alabama Supreme Court. His son Christopher John England, who received his JD from UA, is former chair of the Alabama Democratic Party. Christopher England was the first Black chairman of either major political party in the history of the state of Alabama and serves as a member of the Alabama House of Representatives, representing the 70th District unopposed since 2006.

What UA alum was the first female FBI agent to be sent on assignment outside the United States?

Lois Drolet (1938). She was ordered to Hawaii in 1943, before Hawaii gained statehood.

What UA alum wrote four successful novels and six screenplays for television?

Robert Inman. Novelist, screenwriter, and playwright Robert Inman is a native of Elba, Alabama, where he began his writing career in junior high school with his hometown weekly newspaper. He left a thirty-one-year career in journalism in 1996 to devote himself to creative writing full-time with great success.

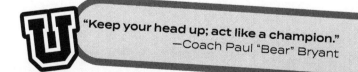

"Keep your head up; act like a champion."
—Coach Paul "Bear" Bryant

What UA alum made history on campus in June 1963, but did not remain long?

Dr. James Hood. Along with Vivian Malone, he was one of the first two African-American students to enroll at UA in 1963 during the "Stand in the School House Door." While he did not complete his undergraduate degree at UA, he returned to earn his doctorate in 1997.

What UA alum was prevented from attending in 1956, but returned to receive a master's degree from UA in 1991?

Autherine Lucy Foster. She received her degree at the same ceremony as her daughter, who earned a bachelor's degree in finance.

What internationally known painter's work was selected by FDR to hang in the White House? What area on campus holds three of his paintings?

Kelly Fitzpatrick (Class of 1910). His works were also hung in Supreme Court justice Hugo Black's office, as well as in the office of Senator John Bankhead. The W. S. Hoole Special Collections Library on the UA campus has three of his paintings in their collections. The paintings are part of a series depicting industries in Alabama.

"The University is the Capstone of higher education in Alabama."
—Dr. George Hutchinson Denny

What UA alum is the first to be chosen as a US astronaut? In what unique way did he earn his degree? Where did he travel in March of 2001?

Serving as a lieutenant colonel in the US Air Force, James M. Kelly was the first UA graduate to be selected as an astronaut. He earned his master's degree in aerospace engineering in 1996 through the QUEST, or Quality University Extended Site Telecourses program, before online learning became so ubiquitous in our world. Kelly piloted the space shuttle *Discovery* on a mission to the International Space Station.

What 1951 UA graduate had a hand in Saturn, Apollo, Skylab, and the Space Shuttle programs, and holds a patent for Rod Peening-Process and Tool Improvement?

Vincent P. Caruso. He was named a Distinguished Fellow of the UA Department of Industrial Engineering in 2000.

What UA alum and friend of Paul "Bear" Bryant was a groundbreaking newspaper owner, a Pulitzer Prize winner, and a civil rights champion?

Hazel Brannon Smith (1935).

What 1999 grad [MFA, creative writing] won the coveted Yale Series of Younger Poets Competition in 2001?

Maurice Manning, for his critically acclaimed collection of poems, *Lawrence Booth's Book of Visions.*

> "Soon as the evening shades prevail,
> The moon takes up the wondrous tale,
> And nightly to the listening earth,
> Repeats the story of her birth;
> While all the stars that round her burn,
> And all the planets in their turn,
> Confirm the tidings as they roll,
> And spread the truth from pole to pole."
> —Joseph Addison, 1672–1719

What MFA in creative writing alum authored a book that was adapted for a television series?

Alissa Nutting. She is a creative writing professor and author, and her book, *Made for Love,* was adapted as a series for HBO Max.

What UA alum's short story "Time's End" appeared in the Best Short Stories of 1943 and had several stories appear in publications such as *American Mercury* and the *Saturday Evening Post*?

Robert P. Gibbons. Gibbons was one of many of Hudson Strode's successful students.

Name the UA alum who served as assistant surgeon general of the United States.

Dr. Ralph C. Williams, a 1910 UA graduate, was appointed to the post in 1943.

Who was the first woman to receive a BA from UA?

Rosa Lawhorn, in 1900.

What UA alum made headlines around the world and has become a symbol of success and triumph for generations to come? What honor was bestowed upon her in 2000?

Vivian Malone Jones. In 1965, she was the first African American to graduate from The University of Alabama. She was given an honorary doctorate in humane letters from UA.

Who was the first woman to receive an MA from UA?

Lida McMahon, in 1902.

What UA alum went on to direct orchestras in places like the Coconut Grove and the Armand Club?

Buddy Clark, who was known at UA as Herbert Kreisberg, Class of 1937.

What UA alum and physician was a pioneer in the use of X-rays?

Dr. Eugene Northington, whose work with the Roentgen ray helped aid the suffering of others, but in turn caused his demise. Northington General Hospital was named in his honor.

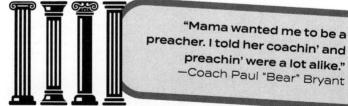

"Mama wanted me to be a preacher. I told her coachin' and preachin' were a lot alike."
—Coach Paul "Bear" Bryant

What two UA alums helped implement the Civil Rights Act of 1964 and the Voting Rights Act of 1965?

Founders of the Southern Poverty Law Center Morris Dees and Joseph J. Levin Jr.

What online open-source encyclopedia and ubiquitous resource was invented by UA graduate Jimmy Wales?

Wikipedia.

In 1987, what did UA graduate Morris Dees and his Southern Poverty Law Center accomplish for client Beulah Mae Donald?

They argued her case against the Klansmen who had lynched her son, Michael, in 1981, and when she won, the courts awarded her $7 million to be paid by The United Klans of America. Since the Klan had nowhere near that amount of money to turn over to Mrs. Donald, she ended up bankrupting the organization and possessing their Alabama headquarters building.

Tom Cherones, who received his MA in broadcast and film communication at UA, directed over eighty episodes of which popular 1990s sitcom about nothing?

Seinfeld. Cherones is best known for his work on *Seinfeld*, where he directed eighty-one of the eighty-six episodes of the first five seasons. Yadda yadda yadda, he won a Directors Guild of America Award, and a Primetime Emmy Award as producer.

LEADERS

Who was the first president of The University of Alabama? Where was he from?

Alva Woods (1831–1837). Vermont—though he was educated in Massachusetts, at Phillips Academy and at Harvard.

What UA president served as the chaplain at the inauguration of Jefferson Davis on February 18, 1861?

Basil Manly (1837–1855). Manly was an ardent secessionist.

Upon leaving his post after eighteen years of presidency, what other Alabama and Southern institutions did Manly help develop?

The Southern Baptist Convention, the Alabama Historical Society, and the Alabama Insane Hospital (later known as Bryce Hospital).

What UA president is believed to have started UA's first musical group?

Landon Cabell Garland (1855–1865). Family tradition says that Garland organized a musical group soon after joining the faculty as a professor in 1847.

Name the UA president who was a member of the University's inaugural class, attending UA from 1831 to 1834.
William Russell Smith (1870–1871).

Which former UA president was the father of the first Auburn football team captain?
Nathaniel Thomas Lupton (1871–1874).

What former UA president was known to have had three horses shot out from under him at Jonesboro during the Civil War? What prompted him to come to The University of Alabama?
Henry Delamar Clayton (1886–1889). An unsuccessful bid for the governorship of Alabama brought him to come to UA to teach international law. He was conferred with an honorary degree of doctor of laws before taking his teaching post.

What UA president was the first University graduate to hold the office of president? What major accomplishments occurred during his presidency?
Burwell Boykin Lewis (1880–1885). He graduated from The University of Alabama in 1857. He was responsible for bringing in funds from the US Congress for war losses, and for rebuilding the campus both physically and psychologically following the Civil War.

In what area did Burwell Boykin Lewis teach?

Constitutional law.

What UA president served less than a year but was renowned as a naval officer and hydrographer, and inventor of the electric torpedo?

Matthew Fontaine Maury. He served only briefly as president in the latter half of 1871.

Which UA professor studied under a famed chemist whose name is immortalized in a piece of chemistry equipment used in every lab around the world?

Nathaniel Thomas Lupton (1871–1874). He studied in Germany under Robert Wilhelm Bunsen, namesake of the "Bunsen burner."

What nineteenth-century UA president left the University to become president of the Normal College for Girls at Livingston (now the University of West Alabama)?

Carlos G. Smith (1874–1878). The Board of Trustees voted not to reappoint him in 1878 and brought about great public controversy.

What UA president served as acting president multiple times before finally accepting the post permanently?
William Stokes Wyman, in 1879–80, 1885–86, and 1889–90. He accepted the appointment as UA president in 1901.

What screen legend was photographed with UA president Richard Clarke Foster on the 1938 Rose Bowl trip?
Humphrey Bogart.

What former UA president served as supervisor of campus construction before becoming president and saw a major building program that continued throughout his tenure as president?
John Morin Gallalee (1948–1953). Nine dormitories, two classroom buildings, and a stadium expansion occurred during his tenure.

> "We, as teachers, coaches, administrators, and students, must understand that success will be determined largely by the hard work, communication, and sacrifice for each other. We are accountable to each other in the classroom, on the playing field, and in the community."
> —Former UA head football coach Mike Shula

"Bryant was a man who embodied our national character. I was a great fan of his."
—Ronald Reagan

Why was The University of Alabama's New College founded in the early 1970s? Who were its first two deans?

It was established as an independent college within the University, embracing interdisciplinary teaching and a smaller liberal arts college feel. Its first two deans were Neal Bertie (1972–1974) and Bernie Sloan (1974–1997). New College thrives to this day!

What two former UA presidents also served as chancellor of Vanderbilt University?

Landon Cabell Garland and Oliver Cromwell Carmichael. Garland is buried on the Vanderbilt campus.

Which president saw the admission of women to The University of Alabama?

Richard Channing Jones (1890–1897).

During the creation of an 1852 map of the UA campus, who served as "chain bearer"?

Then–UA president Basil Manly. He was directly involved in the measuring of campus to ensure the accuracy of the map.

What UA administrator served as the dean of men during the integration of The University of Alabama in 1963?
John L. Blackburn. He began his career at The University of Alabama in 1956 and he became dean of men in 1958. In 1963, his dedication to progress and meticulous planning were credited as key elements in the historic peaceful integration of African Americans into the Capstone. The Blackburn Institute, a leadership development and civic engagement program specifically focused on improving the state of Alabama, is named in his honor.

What former UA president launched the Greater University Building Program, which resulted in the first construction on campus in nearly two decades? What other major endeavor occurred during his tenure?
John William Abercrombie (1902–1911). This plan was launched in 1906. He instituted summer school for teachers at UA, which began in 1904.

Where were the first summer school courses taught?
Outside, under canopies or tents. Enrollment was so great during the second session that many of the male students lived in university-provided tents on campus.

What was the name of Dr. Denny's beloved dog?
Bonnie, a beautiful and faithful collie.

What wife of a former UA president penned a book on the President's Mansion, written from the point of view of the mansion?

Mary Mathews, wife of Dr. David Mathews.

What interesting rule was stated in the UA Board of Trustees Oath of Office, written in 1848?

It states that the trustees were forbidden to take up arms against each other, or against state officials.

Which UA president came to Alabama after a brilliant thirty-five-year career with the University of Texas System?

President Robert E. Witt. His tenure in Texas included ten years as dean of the business school at the University of Texas at Austin, and eight years as president of the University of Texas at Arlington.

> "A major focus of the past academic year at UA has been growth with quality. The cornerstone of our vision for the future is to become a university of choice for the best and brightest. This year that vision became a reality."
> —Then–UA president Robert Witt in his 2005 address to faculty and staff

What rank did UA president Josiah Gorgas hold in the Confederate army? When Gorgas resigned as seventh president of The University of Alabama in 1879, what University post was awarded to him?

Brigadier-General. Gorgas resigned from the presidency for health reasons and was named University librarian. He was succeeded by his wife, Amelia Gayle Gorgas, upon his death.

Who was the youngest president of The University of Alabama? What prestigious position did he accept in 1975 which required him to leave Tuscaloosa for three years?

Dr. David Mathews, who served from 1969 to 1980, and was just thirty-four when he became president. He was named the US Secretary of Health, Education, and Welfare under President Gerald Ford's administration.

What UA president had been the youngest university president in American history?

Dr. Frank Rose (1958–1969), who was president of Transylvania University in Kentucky at age thirty.

"Touch dat thang fo!"
—Courtney Upshaw after the 2012 BCS National Championship. Upshaw was named the defensive MVP with his seven-tackle performance, which included one sack and one tackle for a loss.

What other UA president also served as president of Transylvania University?

UA's first president, Alva Woods (1831–1837).

What former UA leader is an internationally recognized poet?

Dr. Hank Lazer. His works have been published in leading magazines and journals.

What former UA dean wrote the definitive work on the integration of The University of Alabama?

Dean E. Culpepper Clark, author of *Schoolhouse Door: Segregation's Last Stand at The University of Alabama* (Oxford University Press, 1993).

Why segregation's "last stand"?

Alabama was the fiftieth state in the union to integrate its public school system.

Under what president were doctoral degrees first offered at UA?

President John M. Gallalee.

What programs offered the first PhD degrees?

Commerce and business administration, chemistry, education, English, biology, history, physics, political science, anatomy, biochemistry, pharmacology, and physiology.

What University of Alabama president served at two separate times and later became chancellor?

Dr. Denny. He first served The University of Alabama from 1912 to 1937, and then returned upon the death of President Foster in 1941.

The Hoole Library is named for whom?

William Stanley Hoole. Besides directing the University libraries for many years, he authored several books and articles in a myriad of areas, with a special interest in Southern history.

Which University president was responsible for turning The University of Alabama into a military school? In what year? What were his motivations?

President Landon Cabell Garland made UA a military school in 1860, though Garland had begun to make plans for the conversion in 1854. It was done in an attempt to control student behavior. The 1860 student body was made up of all white young men, younger than what we now consider college age, and from privileged backgrounds.

Who was sometimes called the "Angel of the Campus Cadets"? What distinction did she receive in Washington as a young woman?

Amelia Gayle Gorgas. She was one of two women on the platform during the ceremony when the cornerstone of the Washington Monument was laid.

> "I'm always running around. Not all the time do you understand, but you always had my back, you always supported me and for that I'm forever grateful. I'd like to thank the rest of my family also, everyone out there who supported me. I'm super grateful."
> —Alabama quarterback Bryce Young after winning the 2021 Heisman Trophy

What former UA administrative leader single-handedly acquired Moundville to be part of The University of Alabama?

Dr. Walter B. Jones, who at the time was Alabama's state geologist, purchased the land with his own money to assure that it would be saved and studied.

What former UA administrative leader received two major honors relating to Alabama in 2003?

Dr. Malcolm Portera, chancellor of The University of Alabama System. In 2003, he was inducted into the Alabama Academy of Honor, and also received the Governor's Award for Distinguished Service to Alabama from then-governor Bob Riley.

From what institution did Dr. Denny come to The University of Alabama?

He came from Washington and Lee in Virginia in 1912, where he had served as president.

"Ruin seize thee, ruthless Kind!
Confusion on thy banners wait,
Though fann'd by Conquest's crimson wing
They mock the air with idle state."
—Thomas Gray (1716–1771), from *The Bard*

Who was The University of Alabama's first Rhodes Scholar? What major milestone occurred during his presidency?

Oliver Cromwell Carmichael, who went on to graduate from UA in 1911 and returned in 1953 as president of the University until 1957. He was president when Autherine Lucy, the first African-American student to be admitted to UA, came to campus in 1956.

What former UA president was a captain in the Creek War and served in the Congress of the Confederacy as well as the US Congress?

William Russell Smith, who served as UA president briefly in 1870-71.

What year did Lee Bidgood, namesake of Bidgood Hall, begin his role as director of the School of Commerce and Business Administration? What other administrative role did he take on in 1953?

He began that role in 1919. He also served as interim president upon the retirement of President Gallalee.

In what language were the earliest university diplomas written, including the names of the students and faculty?

Latin. Everything was written in Latin!

When was the Graduate School first established? Who was the first dean of the Graduate School?

It was established in 1922 and instituted in 1924. Dr. A. B. Moore served as its first dean.

Who was the first dean of the Law School?

Dean Albert J. Farrah. Farrah Hall, the former Law School building, bears his name.

What two former UA presidents were honored as one of the "Ten Outstanding Young Men in America"?

Dr. Rose, in 1954, and Dr. Mathews, in 1969.

> "They all came to Alabama because they wanted a great education, they wanted to be part of a family environment, and they all wanted to win a national championship."
> —Former UA Women's Gymnastics head coach Sarah Patterson on her 2002 national championship team

What did students raise money for after the death of President Foster in 1941?

An iron lung, a method of treating patients with severe respiratory illness. Students raised more than $1,200, an enormous sum at that time, for an iron lung to be donated to Druid City Hospital in Dr. Foster's name.

What UA president was elected as the president of the State University Association?

President Paty (1942–1947) was elected to that post in 1943.

During President Paty's early years as president, why was the campus so crowded? Why did he leave UA?

Despite low enrollment during wartime, throughout 1943 and 1944, UA housed, fed, and trained—both academically and physically—almost thirteen thousand men in US Army and Navy programs. Dr. Paty left to accept the chancellorship of the University of Georgia System.

How many female students were there when Dr. Denny became president in 1912?

Fifty-five.

"He never knew pain who never felt the pangs of love."
—Samuel P. Thomas, Class of 1906

> **"The primary goal for Mark's Madness is to be as loud and intimidating as possible, but at the same time show the great amount of class that this University and its fans have been known for."**
> —Jay McPhillips, UA student and 2004-05 season president of Mark's Madness, the then–student basketball fan group

What former dean of women and dean of the College of Home Economics was conferred with an LLD degree by the University in 1941 in recognition for her more than three decades of service?

Dean Agnes Ellen Harris.

When was The University of Alabama System created?

In 1975. The UA System is made up of three research universities, as well as a medical center: The University of Alabama (the flagship institution), University of Alabama–Huntsville, and University of Alabama-Birmingham. The UA System is the largest employer in the state of Alabama.

What administrative body oversaw the creation of the System?

The University of Alabama's Board of Trustees.

"My feelings have changed through the years, as I have watched UA push forward in the enrollment and graduation of African-American students, to the point that today it is a national leader among doctoral degree–granting institutions. I have admired even more UA's awareness that it is not where it needs and wants to be on the issues that vitally affect the people of this state, especially its African-American population. But I have confidence today, that I would not have had years ago, that it will succeed."
—Vivian Malone Jones, first African-American graduate of UA, 2000 UA Commencement address

When was the Honors College first established at UA? Who was named its first dean?

In September 2003. Dr. Robert Halli, who oversaw its three divisions: University Honors, Computer-based Honors, and International Honors.

Who was the first woman to serve on UA's Board of Trustees?

Martha Simms Rambo. She was confirmed as a trustee by the Alabama state legislature in 1981. She was also the first woman on the board of the Birmingham branch of the Federal Reserve Bank, and the first recipient of the Virginia Hammill Simms Award for outstanding contributions to the arts.

What UA administrator penned a poignant poem to mark the fortieth anniversary of the integration of The University of Alabama? What did he do to the benefit of the UA community and to Tuscaloosa and Northport?

Dr. Charles Ray Nash, then–vice chancellor for academic affairs for The University of Alabama System. His poem is entitled "Our Future." Dr. Nash initiated the application for Tuscaloosa/Northport to be designated an All-America City, which it received in 2002.

Before being named provost in 2003, what UA college did Provost Judy Bonner serve as dean for fourteen years?

The College of Human Environmental Sciences.

What other distinction sets Judy Bonner apart?

She was the first and only (to date!) woman to serve as president of The University of Alabama.

> "UA is one of the finest institutions of learning in the South, and I am happy to pay tribute to the devotion of the people who have contributed to its success. It is to such institutions that this state and our nation must look for leadership in the years ahead."
> —US senator from Arkansas J. William Fulbright in his 1956 UA Commencement address

What former UA president was instrumental in the establishment of the Alabama Institute for Manufacturing Excellence (AIME)?
Dr. Roger Sayers (1988–1996).

What former UA president was the uncle of a legend in UA sports broadcasting?
President Richard Clarke Foster. His nephew John Forney was known to many as the "Voice of the Crimson Tide."

Who was the first chancellor of The University of Alabama System? What other administrative first did he achieve?
Joseph F. Volker, who became chancellor in 1976. He was the UA's first dean of the School of Dentistry.

When was the Department of Fine Arts officially formed? Who was the first director of the Department of Fine Arts?
In 1943. Dr. Alton O'Steen. The new department combined art, music, and related fields.

"If I should go to sleep for 61 years and wake up in the middle of the Sahara desert, I would feel no more lost than I do now, coming back to UA after 61 years absence."
—Joseph U. Gillespie, Class of 1873, remarking on the changes to the UA

What UA alum and administrator was inducted into the prestigious Alabama Academy of Honor in 2004? Who nominated her, and what other honor do they both share?

Dr. Cathy Johnson Randall. Dr. Randall was nominated for the honor by Harper Lee, fellow UA alum and honoree. The Academy is limited to one hundred living Alabamians plus living governors, and vacancies occur only at the death of a member. Both Randall and Lee have been named among the University's "XXXI Most Outstanding Women Graduates of the Century."

Who served with distinction on the UA faculty and as a department head for nearly twenty years, then left, and then returned to serve as UA president?

Named the twenty-ninth president of UA in 2015, Dr. Stewart Bell previously served the Capstone for sixteen years as a faculty member and then department head of mechanical engineering. With research concentrations in combustion engines, he founded and directed UA's Center for Advanced Vehicle Technologies, an interdisciplinary research center producing new generations of engineers and scientists.

Which of UA's presidents was also a biology professor and co-author of naturalism books including *Wildflowers of Alabama* and *Adjoining States*?

Dr. Joab Thomas (1981–1988). He also served as the president of Penn State University and North Carolina State University.

"We are born to be dynamic and restless and adaptable. We need only to continue to prove it. The future will require that we liberate ourselves from the frozen attitudes and fixed expectations of the past."
—Elmo Ellis, UA alum, from his book *Happiness Is Worth the Effort*

Which spouse of a former UA president has an endowed fund named in her honor, created to strengthen the University libraries' collections on women?

Donna Sorensen. The Endowed Libraries Collection is named for the wife of former UA president Dr. Andrew Sorensen.

TOWN AND GOWN

What Tuscaloosa native won a Grammy award in 1959?
Dinah Washington. The song was "What a Diff'rence a Day Makes!" Washington was born in Tuscaloosa in 1924, but left at age four and moved to Chicago with her family.

What facility is named in her honor in Tuscaloosa?
The Dinah Washington Cultural Arts Center. The CAC is a hub for the arts in Tuscaloosa, and is managed and maintained by the Tuscaloosa Arts Council.

What neighboring venue is a great place to spend an afternoon or an evening?
The historic Bama Theatre. Built in 1938 through funds from the Federal Public Works Administration, the Bama continues to draw audiences for a wide variety of programming and events, with its twinkling lights and beautiful spaces.

What former UA student became the youngest city councilperson in Tuscaloosa history?

Lee Garrison. He was elected in August 1997 to represent District 4 while still an undergraduate at UA.

Who has served the city of Tuscaloosa as its mayor since 2005, taking the city through unprecedented growth as well as unthinkable tragedy?

Walt Maddox. As the city of Tuscaloosa's thirty-sixth mayor, he served during the devastation of the 2011 tornadoes and the complex aftermath, and has worked tirelessly with the community to rebuild and grow his beloved city.

What was Tuscaloosa's first craft brewery, established when state laws changed, in 2012?

Druid City Brewing Company, established by Bo Hicks and Elliott Roberts.

"And just to all the young kids out there that's not the biggest, not the strongest, just keep pushing because I'm not the biggest. I've been doubted a lot just because of my size, and really it just comes down to you put your mind to it, you can do it. No job is too big. If you put your mind to it, you can do it, and just keep believing in God, and you'll get where you want to be."
—from DeVonta Smith's Heisman Trophy acceptance speech

> **"That line is a great one and I'll take my hat off to the boys. The game should be a great one."**
> —Then–Vanderbilt assistant coach Paul "Bear" Bryant on Alabama's football team

What playful nod do they give in their logo to a long-beloved Tuscaloosa symbol?

DCBC's logo is a take on the beloved Moon-Winx Lodge neon sign.

Who designed the original Moon-Winx sign?

Local legend and hero Glenn House, an illustrator, painter, sculptor, papermaker, printer, and student of whatever else caught his eye. He designed the Moon-Winx sign during his first job out of college.

Where did Glenn spend a lot of his time on the UA campus?

In Woods Hall and in Gorgas Library. Glenn helped establish and taught for years in The University of Alabama's MFA Program in Book Arts.

Besides training a wide array of incredibly talented book artists for the past several decades, what is the Book Arts Program's unique distinction?

It was the first graduate-level master's program in the book arts in the United States.

What tree did Glenn harness and teach about, changing the art of papermaking, using local resources?

He popularized Alabama Kozo, made from the inner bark of indigenous paper mulberry trees.

Who was one of Glenn's biggest influences?

Glenn's mother, Lucile Hollingsworth House, better known as "Ma'Cille." She led the family on digging vacations, where art met junking met archaeology. Their discoveries as a family led to the creation in the 1960s of the famously surreal "Ma'Cille's Museum of Miscellanea," a sort of art installation and destination in the community.

What was unique about Northington Hospital when it opened in 1944?

It was the second-largest hospital in the United States for burn victims.

What was Northington Hospital's fate?

It was blown up, quite dramatically, on film.

What film was this explosion used for? What world's record was broken during the filming of that movie?

Hooper (1978), starring Burt Reynolds and Sally Field. The last few minutes were filmed at Northington. A. J. Bakunas, stuntman for Burt Reynolds (who ironically was playing a stuntman in the film), dropped 232 feet, setting a record for the highest jump without a parachute.

What other film that captures fictional life in Tuscaloosa starred Sally Field?

Forrest Gump (1994). It was based on the novel of the same name, written by UA alum Winston Groom.

What Tuscaloosa establishment's nickname was a reflection of the travel time it takes to get there?

Nick's or, as it is affectionately known, "Nick's in the Sticks"—a great place for a steak and a lot of atmosphere.

> "To be successful in student politics at UA, the challenge for us is to field qualified, attractive, appealing candidates, so that means candidate selection and training and officer development are critical to being successful in politics."
> —Cleo Thomas, the first African-American SGA president at UA

What is the specialty drink of the house at Nick's?

The famed Nicodemus, unmistakably bright red, topped with what can only be described as legal moonshine, and a cherry. Not for the faint of heart!

What distinction did Tuscaloosa receive in 2002? In what company was Tuscaloosa for this award?

It was named an "All-America City." Anchorage, Alaska; Fountain, Colorado; Elgin, Illinois; Roswell, New Mexico; Buffalo-Niagara, New York; Huntington, New York; Weslaco, Texas; Hampton, Virginia; and Everett, Washington were also chosen.

What popular Tuscaloosa restaurant and health food store, now situated on McFarland Boulevard across from Snow Hinton Park, was first located on The Strip when it opened in 1980?

Manna Grocery and Deli.

What formerly unused structure that now serves as part of the UA Museums was designed by a student of famed architect Frank Lloyd Wright?

Queen City Pool, located on Jack Warner Parkway (formerly River Road). Its unique round design is unmistakably influenced by Wright's Prairie Style architecture. It is now the Mildred Westervelt Warner Transportation Museum.

> "He set a standard of excellence here in that some say is too high but in my opinion that's not necessarily a bad thing. If you don't play football or any other sport to win, you're not much of a competitor. Yet, team spirit and character are extremely important in athletics but in the end cut through all the clichés and we all play the game to win."
> —Former Bryant Museum director Ken Gaddy on Coach "Bear" Bryant

What Tuscaloosa native became Alabama's first and only female governor?

Lurleen B. Wallace. She was also the first and only spouse of a former Alabama governor to become governor of Alabama.

Whose motto is "Ain't Nothin' Like 'em Nowhere"?

Dreamland Barbeque. And it's true!

What is the oldest church in Tuscaloosa County? What significance does this church hold to The University of Alabama?

First Baptist Church in Tuscaloosa. It was first organized in 1818, and the first buildings were constructed of logs. The church was influenced by the leadership of the first two UA presidents, Alva Woods and Basil Manly, who both often filled the pulpit.

What world-class art collection was once on display in Tuscaloosa?

The Tuscaloosa Museum of Art, previously the Westervelt-Warner Museum of American Art, was an art museum. The museum permanently closed in 2018. The museum was the result of forty years of collecting American art by Tuscaloosa native Jack Warner, CEO of Gulf States Paper, later the Westervelt Company. He founded the museum in 2003 after exhibiting portions of the collection in the headquarters building of the Westervelt Company. The collection contained more than five hundred works by such artists as Whistler, Homer, and Cassatt.

Why is Tuscaloosa known as "The Druid City"?

The name is derived from the presence of many large oak trees in the city. In ancient times the Druids held the oak tree in great reverence and conducted their rituals in oak forests.

Where did Tuscaloosa get its name?

The modern city name, Tuscaloosa, was derived from the old name, Tuskaloosa. In the languages of the Creek and Choctaw Indians, *tushka* means warrior and *lusa* means black.

What is the name of the river that runs through the city?

The Black Warrior River!

What downtown Tuscaloosa church was built in 1829, making it the second oldest of its denomination in the state of Alabama? What is its significance to The University of Alabama?
Christ Episcopal Church, organized January 7, 1828. Charter ceremonies for UA were held in this church and Reverend Alva Woods was installed as the first president of the University on April 12, 1831.

Name the bookstore once located on The Strip that was named for a Tom Robbins novel.
Another Roadside Attraction. It closed in the 1980s.

What Tuscaloosa community leader was the first African American elected to the Tuscaloosa County Commission?
Joseph W. Mallisham.

What once stood on the site of Snow Hinton Park? Who is the park named for?
Northington General Hospital. The park is named for former Tuscaloosa mayor Snow Hinton and definitely not for the weather!

> "I'm a little overwhelmed right now. I'm just so excited to bring Alabama their first Heisman winner."
> —Mark Ingram, in his 2009 Heisman Trophy acceptance speech

Name the man who won a Pulitzer Prize for speaking out against segregation in Tuscaloosa in 1956.

Buford Boone, editor and publisher of the *Tuscaloosa News*. His editorial "What a Price for Peace" was published on February 7, 1956.

What Tuscaloosa church is the oldest Black Presbyterian church in Alabama?

The Brown Memorial Presbyterian Church. It was organized by Dr. Charles A. Stillman as Salem Church in December of 1880.

What is Stillman's namesake in Tuscaloosa?

Stillman College. Stillman is a private, historically Black Presbyterian college and is accredited by the Southern Association of Colleges and Schools.

What was Stillman College originally called?

Stillman College was founded as Tuscaloosa Institute, when it was authorized by the General Assembly of the Presbyterian Church in the United States in 1875, and held its first classes in 1876. It was chartered as a legal corporation by the State of Alabama in 1895. At that time, the name was changed from Tuscaloosa Institute to Stillman Institute.

"They've got one heartbeat, together a team."
—Coach Paul "Bear" Bryant

What Tuscaloosa facility was designed using what is called moral architecture? When was it established? What internationally known humanitarian aided in its establishment?

Bryce Hospital, originally called the Alabama Insane Hospital. Alabama was the first state to appropriate sufficient funds for such a facility in 1852, and it opened in 1861.The linear architecture of the main building of what was to become known as Bryce Hospital served as a model for dozens of mental institutions across the United States.

Dorothea Dix. Bryce and the surrounding campus is now owned by The University of Alabama and is undergoing renovations and adaptations for the future.

What is the oldest scientific agency in the state of Alabama?

The Geological Survey of Alabama, which was established by legislative mandate in 1848. Its offices are on the UA campus.

Who built the first bridge spanning the Black Warrior River between Tuscaloosa and Northport?

The first bridge was built in 1834 by Horace King, who at that time was enslaved. King engineered the third bridge in 1872. He had been freed in 1846 and had become a well-known bridge builder in Alabama and Georgia.

What happened to the first bridge? What was the fate of the second bridge?

It was destroyed by a tornado in 1842. Replaced by a new bridge built in 1852, it was defended by Tuscaloosa Home Guard before its destruction by Federal troops in April 1865.

What innovation in 1943 made travel to the Alabama capital of Montgomery much easier?

The opening of the "University Highway," which is now US 82. This route connected Montgomery to Tuscaloosa and took approximately fifty miles off of the trip between the two cities.

What manufacturing facility in Tuscaloosa is the largest of its kind outside of its native country?

The Mercedes-Benz plant, which was established in Tuscaloosa in 1994 and underwent a $600 million expansion in 2000. It is one of the largest employers in Alabama.

What's the "Crazy Bucket"?

A signature drink at famed Tuscaloosa watering hole Harry's Bar, which was established in 1979.

What former US congressperson and US ambassador to New Zealand, Fiji, Tonga, and Western Samoa once practiced law in Tuscaloosa?

Armistead Selden Jr.

> **"These students will remain on campus. They will register today. They will go to school tomorrow."**
> —Deputy Attorney General Nicholas Katzenbach, in reference to Vivian Malone and James Hood, to George Wallace at Foster Auditorium, 1963

What corporation headquartered in Tuscaloosa was founded in 1884?

Gulf States Paper Corporation. It was one of the nation's largest privately held forest products companies.

Who started his first newspaper, the *Alabama Citizen*, in Tuscaloosa in 1943 and soon became one of Alabama's preeminent newspaper publishers?

Frank Thomas. In 1972, Thomas was the first African American inducted into the Alabama Newspaper Hall of Honor in recognition of his efforts to promote the advancement of civil rights, understanding, and racial harmony in Alabama.

What Tuscaloosa institution opened in 1956 and closed its doors for the last time on Halloween of 2003? What words were painted outside the building for many years?

The Chukker, a legendary Tuscaloosa hangout. "Liberte, Egalite, Fraternite! Vive le Chukker—1956."

"There is nothing unpatriotic about remaining in college—on the contrary, it is the highest form of patriotism to prepare oneself to render some really worthwhile service in time of need."
—Dr. Denny on military service versus college study, 1941

Name the Tuscaloosa city councilperson who has hosted a local television program?

Kip Tyner, and his show, *Great Day Tuscaloosa!*

What major fundraiser (and creative masterpiece) takes place in Tuscaloosa annually, raising thousands for WAAO (West Alabama Aids Outreach)? When does it take place?

The annual Bal Masque. During Mardi Gras season, just before Fat Tuesday.

What "local meat and three" has fried green tomatoes only on Tuesdays and Thursdays?

City Cafe—a downtown Northport staple that has been feeding hungry UA students and the Tuscaloosa community for decades.

What Tuscaloosa restaurant chain will celebrate its fiftieth anniversary in 2024?

Taco Casa—known not only for its great food, but also for its great ice.

Who founded Taco Casa?

Rod Wilkin. He played football for the Tide!

What annual event unites the University community and the Tuscaloosa community to celebrate spring?

The annual Sakura Festival—Sakura is a Japanese festival of cherry blossoms, and has been celebrated in Tuscaloosa since 1986. It is organized by the Japan Program, part of UA's Capstone International Programs.

What Japanese manufacturing corporation has a plant in Tuscaloosa?

JVC. The people at JVC were instrumental in establishing the Sakura Festival.

What self-proclaimed UA football "head" cheerleader ran for public office thirteen times, including several bids for governor, and lost them all? What was the name of his book, published in 1980?

Shorty Price. *Shorty: I Ain't Nothing but a Loser.*

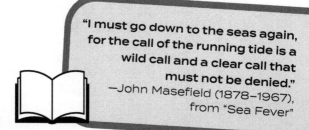

"I must go down to the seas again, for the call of the running tide is a wild call and a clear call that must not be denied."
—John Masefield (1878–1967), from "Sea Fever"

What major newspaper company now owns the *Tuscaloosa News*?

The *New York Times.*

Who is "The Bronze Bomber" and what accolade did he receive in 2022?

Tuscaloosa native Deontay Wilder is known as "The Bronze Bomber" for winning a bronze medal in the 2008 Olympics! He was honored with a seven-foot-tall statue! The former heavyweight boxing champion unveiled his own statue to hundreds of fans outside the Tuscaloosa Tourism and Sports building. Wilder's incredible record of ten consecutive defenses of his title ties Wilder with Muhammad Ali for fifth all-time among heavyweights.

Who is the artist that created the statue?

Tuscaloosa artist Caleb O'Connor. His works can be seen in Tuscaloosa and elsewhere, including a beautiful sculpture of Minerva at the Park at Manderson Landing, unveiled in 2019 in honor of Tuscaloosa's bicentennial, marking two hundred years since the city's incorporation on December 13, 1819.

> **"UA is proud of its alumni. Day by day, all over this nation and on the battlefronts of the world, the sons and daughters of the University are adding greatly to its glory through distinguished careers of social usefulness."**
> —Raymond R. Paty, UA president, 1943

What is the largest outdoor theater in West Alabama and a great place to see and hear a concert?

The Tuscaloosa Amphitheater, near the banks of the Black Warrior River. Located only minutes away from The University of Alabama campus, this is a premier location for arts and entertainment. *Alabama Magazine* voted the Tuscaloosa Amphitheater as the No. 1 amphitheater in the state for the 2018 "Best of Bama" awards. In addition to its many great concerts, the amphitheater also hosts the annual Celebration on the River, a free July 4th celebration featuring the Tuscaloosa Symphony Orchestra.

What must-do activity in October can help fill your house with beauty and creativity, and your stomach with fried Twinkies?

The Kentuck Festival of the Arts. Kentuck has a history of over half a century, and is a nationally known crossroads of creativity and community. The two-day festival each October has its roots in folk art and features nearly three hundred artists, as well as live music, spoken word, activities for children, folk and contemporary craft demonstrations, food trucks, and local craft brews.

What is the name of the synagogue in Tuscaloosa that has been active for over one hundred years?

Temple Emanu-El.

What geographic distinction does it have?

It is physically connected with the Bloom Hillel Center for Jewish Student Life on The University of Alabama campus, which recently expanded beyond its original footprint when it was built in 2011, doubling its space to accommodate UA's robust Jewish student population. This distinction makes worship and activities relating to Jewish culture united through the University and the greater community!

Who designed the Bama Theatre and what is it based upon?

The Bama was designed in 1938 by architect D. O. Whilldin, and it was styled as a "reproduction of the courtyard of the Davanzati Palace in Florence, Italy" (not Florence, Alabama!). The orchestra and balcony sections are decorated as a "Spanish Courtyard."

CAMPUS

What was the first permanent structure on The University of Alabama campus? In what year was it built?
The Gorgas House. 1828, as part of the original master plan for The University of Alabama.

Who designed the original architectural plan for the campus of The University of Alabama?
William Nichols. Influenced by Thomas Jefferson's plan at the University of Virginia, the campus featured a seventy-foot-high domed rotunda building that served as the library and nucleus of the campus.

Two facilities, buildings, a playground, and a street are named for the beloved son of a former UA football coach. Who was he?
John Mark "Johnny" Stallings. Two facilities at The University of Alabama were named in honor of Johnny: the Stallings Center (home to the RISE School) and the equipment room in The University of Alabama football building. John Mark's courage and attitude had a positive impact on all who came in contact with him. He also deeply affected Coach Stallings's perception of football, and the coach's approach on the field.

From what other campus did Nichols gain inspiration?

He borrowed from his own work designing the campus for the University of North Carolina–Chapel Hill.

What is the only structure on campus that survives from the 1828 master plan of architect William Nichols?

The Gorgas House.

What was the first function of what is now known as the Gorgas House? What was the Gorgas House built with?

It was originally called "the hotel" and was a dining hall for students. Bricks. These bricks had been used as ballast for English ships that sailed to America and then returned home with Alabama cotton.

When did the Gorgas House first become associated with the Gorgas family? For how many years did a member of the Gorgas family live in this building?

In 1879, when Josiah Gorgas resigned as seventh University of Alabama president due to poor health, he and his family moved into what was then called the "Pratt House" rent-free. Members of the Gorgas family lived in the building for sixty-five years, with the last surviving child of the Gorgases, Maria Gorgas, living in the house until 1954.

What was the first campus building to be completed after the Civil War?

"The Barracks"—now known as Woods Hall, named for first UA president Alva Woods. It uses many bricks salvaged from the original campus buildings.

In what year was the building formerly known as Morgan Hall built? In what year was it renamed?

1911. The name Morgan was removed in 2020, and until a permanent, new name is established, the building is called the English Building.

In what year did The University of Alabama first begin offering summer school?

1904.

How many students enrolled in The University of Alabama in Fall of 2022?

38,645. 42.1 percent of those students come from Alabama, and 57.9 percent come from elsewhere in the United States and internationally. UA is classified as a Tier-1 Research University, which is a designation as a high research focused university, with only the top 2.5 percent of higher education institutions falling into that category.

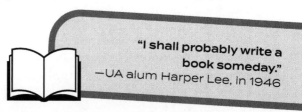

"I shall probably write a book someday."
—UA alum Harper Lee, in 1946

> "Access to [Saban's] program in general has been great. [I can look] out my office window straight over to the football offices. I could walk to his office in a minute. For me not to take advantage of that, I would be a complete idiot. I'm going to take advantage of that as much as possible."
> —Alabama Men's Basketball coach Nate Oats

How many foreign countries are currently represented in The University of Alabama's student enrollment?

Eighty-eight foreign countries!

How many Rhodes Scholars have come from The University of Alabama?

Sixteen! Nick Hayes is the most recent Rhodes Scholar. Hayes was an honors student majoring in German and mathematics.

What Alabama Museum of Natural History-produced program was nominated for an Emmy award in 2005?

Discovering Alabama. Dr. Doug Phillips, originator, producer, and host of the series, and Roger Reid, production coordinator, were nominated for their efforts in developing the episode entitled "Black Belt, Part I."

In what year did The University of Alabama open?
1831.

In what year was Denny Chimes built and dedicated?
1929.

What is "The Capstone"?
Shortly after Dr. George H. Denny became president of The University of Alabama in 1912, he began referring to the school as the state's "capstone" of higher education. Dr. Denny believed in the relationships between all levels of schooling. He viewed the University as the top of an educational structure that began with elementary and high schools across the state and reached all the way to the Tuscaloosa campus. And the name Capstone stuck!

What college at UA uses the Capstone moniker?
The Capstone College of Nursing!

What is special about the trees that line University Boulevard along the side of the Quad?
These trees were planted as a memorial in 1921 by the Tuscaloosa post of the American Legion for those from Tuscaloosa who died in World War I. The plaques are gone, but the trees are registered with the National Forestry Service in Washington, DC.

What was the "Union Building"?

Now known as Reese-Phifer Hall and used by the College of Communication and Information Sciences, the Union Building was built and dedicated in 1930 as "a memorial to all former University of Alabama students who have borne arms in defense of their country."

On what other facility was the original Denny Stadium modeled?

The Yale Bowl.

How many seats did the original stadium hold?

12,072.

What did students do when they saw the elderly Gorgas sisters on campus?

Men would bow and women would curtsey.

"My football training under Wade, plus my experience since boyhood in the hunting and outdoor life of Alabama are undoubtedly responsible for the fact I am alive today."
—Hugh Barr Miller, Class of 1932, on his miraculous rescue after the sinking of the destroyer *The Strong* in 1943

What two women were credited with rescuing campus buildings from the fires set by Federal troops in 1865?

Mrs. Landon Garland, who saved the President's Mansion (which was her family's home), and Mrs. Reuben Chapman, who pleaded for the Observatory to be spared.

Name the four buildings that survived the burning by Union troops.

The Gorgas House, the Observatory, the President's Mansion, and the Little Round House.

What distinction did the Observatory have?

It was the largest observatory east of the Mississippi.

Who were "Miss Julia's Girls"?

Members of the first class of resident women.

When was the first residence hall for women opened?

In 1899. Called the Julia Tutwiler Annex, it housed just ten female students.

Who was the guest performer at the first Rev. Dr. Martin Luther King Jr. Memorial "Realizing the Dream" Concert in 1989?

The actor James Earl Jones.

> "That's how UA won the Rose Bowl game—not by any one player but by teamwork. That's the way the state of Alabama will win, by teamwork and cooperation."
> —Governor Bibb Grave, 1935

Who was buried in the University's cemetery?

At least two enslaved individuals, named Jack and Boysey, both listed as "belonging to" then-president Basil Manly; a student, William J. Crawford, who died of typhus fever in 1844; and the family of former UA professor Horace S. Pratt. Another student, Samuel James, was buried there in 1839, but his body was later disinterred.

Which glam rocker, one of the first openly gay rock stars, performed his last concert (to four encores) in 1974 in Morgan Auditorium?

Jobriath (born Bruce Wayne Campbell), a primary influence on the glam rock characters depicted in the 1998 film *Velvet Goldmine*.

Which 1995 movie with a title referencing The University of Alabama starred Denzel Washington, Gene Hackman, and a submarine?

Crimson Tide.

Why did the movie have that name?
Because the submarine it depicts is the USS *Alabama*. The captain of the submarine also has a dog named Bear, after you-know-who!

Speaking of pets, what 2002 film featured a character whose pet was named for Coach Bryant? What other celebrity animal named "Bear" was named after Coach Bryant?
Sweet Home Alabama. The other "Bear" was the chimp in the 1970s hit TV show *B. J. and the Bear*. It was revealed on an episode that B. J. named his pal in honor of the legendary UA football coach Bear Bryant.

According to Alabama folklorist Kathryn Tucker Windham, whose ghost haunts Smith Hall, which houses the Alabama Museum of Natural History?
The founder of the museum and namesake of the building, geologist Eugene Allen Smith (1841–1927), is said to visit from time to time.

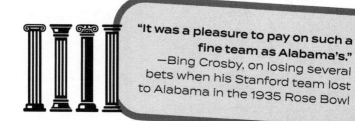

"It was a pleasure to pay on such a fine team as Alabama's."
—Bing Crosby, on losing several bets when his Stanford team lost to Alabama in the 1935 Rose Bowl

When was the military structure of the University abolished?

March 3, 1903. This was initiated by a rebellion that took place in December of 1900 where most of the students enrolled at UA demanded the removal of the military structure and system.

How many telephones were there on campus in 1955?

There were 321 phones across campus. How times have changed!

When was the President's Mansion erected? How much did it cost to build?

1841. The building cost a whopping $18,000 to build.

When were women first enrolled at UA? What was their status that first year?

The fall of 1893. They were considered "special students" rather than regular students.

Who were the first two female students?

Miss Anna Byrne Adams and Miss Bessie Parker, both from Tuscaloosa.

By 1900, how many female students were enrolled at UA?

Twenty-eight.

"When I arrived here, years of preparation had gone into making it happen. I had been active in my own community's efforts to end segregation. . . . I then studied for two years at Alabama A&M, before answering the call that would lead me to the schoolhouse door at this University, where, two years later, I would become its first African-American graduate. Thirty-five years ago, by attending UA, I had the privilege of representing all those who fought for simple justice."
—Vivian Malone Jones, the first African-American graduate of UA

Who was the leading crusader to make The University of Alabama coeducational? Who was her father?

Julia S. Tutwiler. Her father, Henry Tutwiler, was one of the first professors hired for the opening of The University of Alabama.

What did Professor Tutwiler teach?

Ancient languages.

When did men and women first live together in the same dorm complex on campus?

In the fall of 1970, Mary Burke Hall East was converted to a men's dorm, and Mary Burke West remained a women's dorm.

When The University of Alabama was founded in 1831, what was the population of what was then known as Tuskaloosa?

1,068 people inhabited the area, which was accessible only by roads and by water. There was no railroad at the time.

How many locations were considered for The University of Alabama?

Twelve originally, and five in the final ballot (Tuscaloosa, Montevallo, Lagrange, Athens, Belfont). Tuscaloosa received forty-seven out of eighty-one votes from the state legislature.

What was the name of the chosen site?

The chosen site for The University of Alabama campus was known as Marr's Spring, located on what was known in the 1820s as Huntsville Road.

What building was dramatically and intentionally destroyed by an explosion on July 4, 2022, to a cheering audience and livestream?

The women's dormitory, Tutwiler Hall. All thirteen floors, gone in about twenty-four seconds.

Who was Marr's Spring named for?

Judge Marr, who occupied and farmed the land that was to become the campus. He lived in a house where Gorgas House now stands. Marr's Spring still exists on campus behind the Ferguson Center and near ten Hoor Hall.

Where were the materials acquired for the first UA campus buildings?

Sandstone was quarried locally, some bricks were made on site, and the lumber was milled from UA's own timber tract.

What is the claim to fame of the Hodges Meteorite, on display at UA's Alabama Museum of Natural History?

It is the only meteorite known to have struck a human being (Ann Elizabeth Hodges of Sylacauga, Alabama). She sustained a large bruise on her hip, but no permanent physical damage.

Which legendary rock star started his 1990 UA homecoming concert in Coleman Coliseum by announcing that since he was in Alabama, he should sing some Hank Williams?

Bob Dylan.

"I'm at a stage in my career [where] I'm not looking for a stepping-stone to my next job. I'm looking for a capstone, and I can't think of a better capstone to an academic career than the flagship university of the state of Alabama."
—Dr. Robert Witt, on being named president of UA in 2003

Which Hank Williams song did he perform?
"Hey Good Lookin'."

How often do Denny Chimes sound? What tune do the chimes play?
Every fifteen minutes. "Westminster Peal," the same as Big Ben in London.

How many steps are there in Denny Chimes? How many flights of stairs?
Ninety-two. Thirteen.

When was air-conditioning first installed on campus? What building had the first air-conditioning?
August 1953. Gorgas Library.

What was the original appropriation of funds for the first University of Alabama Library?
$6,000 in 1830. It was the largest library in the South prior to the Civil War.

Name the first student officially enrolled in The University of Alabama.
Silas L. Gunn.

How many students were enrolled when UA first opened?

Fifty-two.

How many professors were on hand to teach them?

Four.

When was the ceremony held to open The University of Alabama? Where was it held?

April 12, 1831, at Christ Episcopal Church in downtown Tuscaloosa.

How did the ceremony culminate?

Alabama governor Samuel B. Moore spoke and then delivered the keys to The University of Alabama to Alva Woods, UA's first president.

Where was The University of Alabama School of Medicine originally located?

Mobile.

What seated US president visited the UA campus as part of an election campaign? Where did he eat lunch after his speech?

Ronald Reagan. He visited in October of 1984 as part of his re-election campaign tour. He spoke to nine thousand people on the UA campus. McDonald's in Northport. He had a Big Mac, large fries, and an iced tea.

What myth is represented on the eighteenth-century wallpaper at the University Club?
Cupid and Psyche.

When did UA first offer "distance education"?
In 1919, with the founding of the "Extension Division."

What UA campus building was designated a National Historic Landmark in 2005? What two major campus activities took place there for decades?
Foster Auditorium, the site of George Wallace's "Stand" and the place where Vivian Malone and James Hood registered for classes in June 1963, finally integrating The University of Alabama. The two major activities of registration and graduation took place at Foster, the first and last campus career milestones for students!

What other activities took place in Foster?
It was designed as a multipurpose facility, and it has been just that—concerts, dances, sporting events, and lectures have all taken place there over the years.

> "Her head is surrounded with a halo. In her left hand is an olive branch. Her right hand, holding a pair of compasses, rests upon a globe. Lying at her feet on the left side, are a scroll and a book."
> —A description of the UA seal, 1872

What do Gorgas Library and Foster Auditorium have in common? How was this accomplished?

Both Foster and Gorgas are WPA buildings—constructed as part of President Roosevelt's New Deal. Very few campus buildings were built as WPA projects. Dr. Denny, along with Dr. Foster and the future US senator from Florida and UA alum Claude Pepper, visited Roosevelt in the White House, and explained that UA needed a library because the old one was "burned by the Yankees." UA eventually got the funding.

How was this story disseminated?

By President Roosevelt himself, who regaled America with the tale during one of his famous fireside chats.

What was Emphasis? What was the Emphasis controversy of 1970?

A student-organized speaker series that ran successfully in the late 1960s and early 1970s. Speakers included Robert F. Kennedy, William Kunstler, Dick Gregory, and Madalyn Murray O'Hair. Other controversial speakers were banned from campus, including Abbie Hoffman, of the infamous Chicago Seven, who was banned from speaking alongside George Wallace. A court battle ensued.

What was Experimental College?

A student-run college at UA that offered free courses, including classes in soccer, folk, rock, blues, euthanasia, and much more. Nearly one thousand students took these classes.

> **"I went way beyond that day at that point in my mind. My vision was of the future and graduating and going to classes, things like that."**
> —Vivian Malone Jones, on her experience confronting George Wallace on June 11, 1963

What was "Little Bo"?

The snack bar on the ground floor of Woods Hall.

What was the first Greek letter fraternity to establish a chapter at UA? Where were the first members initiated?

Delta Kappa Epsilon, in 1847. They were initiated at the old Indian Queen Hotel by Charles Foote of DKE's Phi chapter at Yale College.

What was the nickname for the original DKE house?

Built in 1916, it was known as "The Mansion on the Hill."

What was the first Greek letter sorority to establish a UA chapter? What other firsts does this sorority hold?

Kappa Delta was established at UA in 1904. The Zeta chapter of Kappa Delta is the first sorority to have a chapter in the state of Alabama. It is now the oldest continuous chapter in the United States.

What campus dormitory was destroyed by fire in January 1935? Who was the building named for?

Gorgas Hall. It was named for William Crawford Gorgas, the son of Amelia and Josiah Gorgas.

What is General William Crawford Gorgas best known for? Besides saving countless lives, what monumental engineering achievement was completed due to Gorgas's medical work?

As a medical doctor and surgeon general for the US Army, he was largely responsible for the eradication of yellow fever, an overwhelming killer in the nineteenth century. The completion of the Panama Canal.

When did UA's College of Commerce and Business Administration begin?

In January 1920. Within one year, 167 students were enrolled in business courses at UA.

What fraternity, now the largest social fraternity in North America, was founded on The University of Alabama campus in 1956? What is the fraternity's nickname?

Sigma Alpha Epsilon. "Mother Mu."

What is the "Order of the Coif"?

A prestigious national academic honor society for legal education. UA's was established in 1970. Good grades, not good hair, are required.

What groundbreaking UA college was founded that same year?

New College, founded under then-president David Mathews.

What is New College?

Begun as an experiment, it is an innovative and successful interdisciplinary college for motivated and intelligent students at UA, which allows them to develop their own major and take control over their coursework and educational path.

Name the prestigious writers series held at UA.

The Bankhead Writers Series, endowed by the Bankhead Foundation.

What was the quad sometimes used for from 1893 to 1914?

It was the site of Alabama football games before the University Field was established.

In what year was the first section of Denny Stadium completed?

1929. It opened on September 28 of that year.

In what year was the stadium renamed Bryant–Denny?

Coach Bryant's name was added in 1975.

As of fall 2004, what was the seating capacity in Bryant-Denny Stadium? How about today?

Bryant-Denny had 83,818 seats—more than enough to provide a seat for every man, woman, and child in the city limits. Today there are 101,821 seats, and it could still use some more!

What building on campus was evacuated to house the National Defense League?

Woods Hall. It was converted after Dunkirk, in 1941.

What was cut by 30 percent on campus in 1941?

Power! As a war effort to conserve energy, power was cut off on campus from 7:30 p.m. until 4:30 a.m. each day.

What was "Mad Wednesday"? What stunning outcome of "Mad Wednesday" marked a first on campus?

May 13, 1970, was a day of conflict on campus between pro- and anti-administration students. As a result, final exams were made optional.

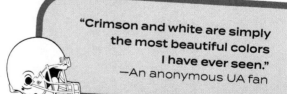

"Crimson and white are simply the most beautiful colors I have ever seen."
—An anonymous UA fan

In what year were the Department of Radio and the Department of Journalism combined?

They were combined in 1973 to form what was then called the School of Communication, now known as the College of Communication and Information Sciences.

What was Dressler Hall? What was its fate?

An intramural sports building on campus. It burned to the ground during student demonstrations in 1970.

What other program, the only one of its kind in the state of Alabama, began in 1970?

The graduate program in Library and Information Studies. Undergraduate work was already a long tradition in librarianship, but UA's master's program started in 1970.

> "I love the University. I have given my life to it. Someday I hope to write its history. I am a fatalist enough, and old enough to be resigned to my fate whatever it may be. But I hope that I shall never be so old, or so fatalist that I will not fight for any battle affecting the University. I will not stand on the sidelines but will enter the fight, and enjoy it."
> —President George H. Denny at the alumni banquet, 1935

What was the theme for the 125th Anniversary of The University of Alabama, held during the 1956–57 academic year?
Teaching, Research, and Service.

What was originally housed in the Rotunda? What was its fate? When was the Rotunda site discovered?
An auditorium on the first floor, and the campus library on the second floor. It was burned to the ground by Union troops in April 1865. In 1894, when workers were laying underground cable. The footprint of the building was just a few inches below ground level.

When did the burning of the UA campus take place?
On April 4, 1865, just five days before Lee's surrender at Appomattox.

What dubious distinction does The University of Alabama have that no other state university can claim?
It was the only one in the country to have been nearly destroyed by enemy action during wartime.

The charred remains of what three books were found in an excavation of the UA campus?
Shakespeare's *Much Ado About Nothing*, *Plane Geometry*, and *Geography of Africa*. The books were found where Madison Hall once stood.

What book was purported to have been rescued from the fire in the Rotunda when the campus was burned by Federal troops in 1865? Was this really the only book that survived the fire? Who was the librarian at the time?

An 1853 edition of the Koran. In 2005, the book was loaned to the Smithsonian for an exhibition. In fact, more than twelve hundred library books survived from different parts of campus. Andre DeLoffre was the librarian, and he remained at his post through the invasion.

What was the Rotunda modeled after? On what classical building are both of these rotundas designed?

William Nichols modeled it loosely after Thomas Jefferson's rotunda at the University of Virginia. They are based on the Roman Pantheon, which was constructed in AD 18–25.

Where is the only known photograph of the Rotunda and the antebellum campus housed? When was that photograph taken?

In the W. S. Hoole Special Collections Library on the UA campus. It is believed to have been taken in 1859 and shows the Rotunda and two dormitories, along with a large number of trees.

Where were classes first taught at UA?

The building was called the Lyceum and it served as the principal classroom building.

> "The people across the state of Alabama are sensing what we sense here on campus—momentum, a growing sense of pride, a growing sense of excitement. We have a very clear vision of what we want UA to be, and we have the commitment and the people to turn that vision into a reality."
> —Former UA President Witt, 2004

Once affixed to a boulder on the quad, what was removed in 2020 and rehoused in Special Collections?

Removed in 2020, a plaque, one of three plaques honoring Confederate students, was authorized for removal by The University of Alabama Board of Trustees.

What were the names of the first dormitories?

Washington and Jefferson Halls.

What exotic import landed on campus during World War II? Why were they in Tuscaloosa? What did many of them take home?

A detachment of French cadets. They were brought to Tuscaloosa to learn how to fly, selected from the French North African Army. Many of those cadets met women and brought home new brides to France. By some accounts, more than eighty Alabama women married French cadets.

When did the Hillel Foundation establish its headquarters on the UA campus? Who was the first director of Hillel at UA?

In 1934. Rabbi Samuel Cook.

Name the UA handyman and janitor who worked with students for three decades, helping with their chemistry work, and on his own experimented with developing fibers using local plants.

Sam S. May, known to students as "Dr. Sam," worked at UA from 1911 until his death in 1941.

What program at UA was one of the first five of its kind in the United States?

Engineering. It began offering classes in 1837, just six years after the university opened its doors.

Name five novels that have depicted The University of Alabama.

Eating the Cheshire Cat by Helen Ellis; *Stars Fell on Alabama* by Carl Carmer; *Wonderdog* by Inman Majors; *Tuscaloosa* by W. Glasgow Phillips; and *Forrest Gump* by Winston Groom. And there are certainly more!

What was the name of Alexandra Robbins's 2004 book in which the author went undercover as a sorority member at several universities, including UA?

Pledged: The Secret Life of Sororities.

"They're sore losers because they're not Alabama."
—From Irvin Carney's epic Tennessee Hate Week Rant

What UA program, conceived of in 1972 and launched in 1975, was the first in the Southeast?

UA's Department of Women's Studies. The program began offering MA degrees in 1988.

What UA institution, which celebrated its 100th anniversary in 2005, has a name that is based on one of their products? Where was it originally located?

The SUPE Store. The University of Alabama's Supply Store had a lunch counter and served soup. The name evolved from there. In the Union building, now known as Reese-Phifer Hall.

Which two very different world-famous New York dance companies conduct summer workshops on the UA campus?

The American Ballet Theatre and the Radio City Music Hall Rockettes. The American Ballet Theatre's workshop at UA is the only one held outside of New York or in partnership with a university.

Which fictional Alabama lawyer lent his name to the UA Law Library online catalog?

The catalog is named ATTICUS after Atticus Finch, the hero of *To Kill a Mockingbird* by UA graduate Harper Lee.

Before being known as the College of Human Environmental Sciences, what was the college called?

The School of Home Economics.

What unlikely department was once under the umbrella of Home Economics?

The Art Department.

How many buildings are on The University of Alabama campus as of 2022?

Nearly three hundred! 297 buildings and counting. With a continually growing campus, there is 10.6 million square feet of space to accommodate all the work and activities across this diverse and dynamic institution.

> "Certainly the virus against which he had warned me was by that time in my veins and I had learned to live the Alabama way. I knew what to expect of the people and what they expected of me. I believe that many had even forgotten I was a Yankee."
> —Carl Carmer, from his book *Stars Fell on Alabama* (Farrar and Reinhart, 1934)

What building was renamed and dedicated to the first African-American faculty member in 2021?

Moore Hall became Archie Wade Hall in 2021, in honor of Dr. Archie Wade. Due to his love of sports, Archie Wade, EdD, retired University of Alabama (UA) professor, is often referred to as the "Jackie Robinson" of the sprawling Tuscaloosa, Alabama, campus. For Wade, the nickname has a deeper meaning: "Breaking down barriers just like the sports legend."

What other building, a center for student life was renamed in 2021?

The UA Student Center was renamed from Ferguson Hall, or "the Ferg," which was named after former trustee William Hill Ferguson who opposed desegregation.

SPORTS

What former UA basketball star was known nationally for his red shoes, or "crimson slippers"?

Antoine Pettway. The beloved player has been on the coaching staff for Alabama Men's Basketball since 2008! As a player, and an undergraduate, he was an integral part of Alabama's NCAA quarterfinal run in 2004, starting every game at point guard. That season marked the third consecutive season in which he led the Tide to the NCAA Tournament. Pettway got his start in coaching while attending graduate school at UA in 2005-06.

Who is credited as giving Paul "Bear" Bryant his first houndstooth hat, which remains an icon to this day? By what moniker is he best known?

Mel Allen, UA alum (1932 and 1936) and lifelong friend of Coach Bryant. As "the voice of the New York Yankees."

Where did Allen and Bryant meet?

They both were students at The University of Alabama in the 1930s.

> "When Sarina rode the royal float into Bryant-Denny stadium, ninety thousand faces would see her time had come at last. The day would mean more than a new dress for another special occasion. Her life would change forever. New doors would open. Old challenges pass."
> —from *Eating the Cheshire Cat*, a novel by Hellen Ellis (Scribner, 2000)

Who are the four Alabama Heisman winners (to date!)

Mark Ingram, running back, 2009; Derrick Henry, running back, 2015; DeVonta Smith, wide receiver, 2020; and Bryce Young, quarterback, 2021.

What baseball Hall of Famer began the 1920 season at UA as team captain?

Joe Sewell.

What future US president entertained the 1938 UA Rose Bowl team on their visit to Hollywood?

Ronald Reagan, who was, at that time, an actor in Hollywood.

Who is the Men's College Basketball coach who got his start at UA before playing thirteen seasons in the NBA?

Maurice "Mo" Williams. He currently coaches Men's Basketball at Jackson State University, in his hometown of Jackson, Mississippi.

What is the CAVE?
The Coleman Auxiliary Volleyball Extension—an expansion of Coleman Coliseum that opened in 1996 and houses the UA volleyball team.

Name the former UA defensive tackle turned entrepreneur who ate forty-three slices of pizza to raise money to fight cystic fibrosis.
Bob Baumhower, whose name in Tuscaloosa brings to mind both football and wings! And pizza!

What year was the first UA Annual Cheerleader Reunion held?
In 1976, after the Alabama versus Southern Mississippi game.

What well-known British actor and comedian visited Tuscaloosa in 2002 and filmed a bit for his HBO show in Bryant-Denny Stadium?
Sacha Baron Cohen. He appeared as his Austrian TV reporter character, Bruno, in the segment.

What Bama football player did he interview?
Shaud Williams, who was an incredibly gracious interviewee given the circumstances.

What year was the first University of Alabama football team formed? Who did UA play? What was the final score?
1892. Birmingham High School. 56-0.

What UA football legend appeared as himself on *The Simpsons* and *The Brady Bunch,* proving both lasting power and his place as an American icon?

Former UA quarterback Joe Namath! Broadway Joe's face and his name are as recognizable today as they were when he played with the Tide in the 1960s.

How many national championships in football has the Crimson Tide won?

The University of Alabama is home to eighteen national championships in football, the most of any school in the Southeastern Conference and among the most in the country. Alabama most recently won the national title in 2020 under Coach Nick Saban.

Name the years.

1925, 1926, 1930, 1934, 1941, 1961, 1964, 1965, 1973, 1978, 1979, 1992, 2009, 2011, 2012, 2015, 2017, and 2020!

How many of those national championships were won by Coach Paul "Bear" Bryant?

Coach Bryant led Alabama to six national championships, the most of any coach at that time. He was tied by Coach Saban for UA national championships under his leadership in 2020. Nick Saban currently holds the record, with seven national titles as a head coach, the most in college football history. One of those championships was as head coach for LSU.

Who was the youngest head coach of the Crimson Tide football program?

Wallace Wade, who was hired in 1923 at the age of thirty-one.

Who was the youngest football coach hired in Alabama's modern era?

Mike Shula. Alabama's twenty-sixth head coach was thirty-eight years old when hired in 2003. Mike played for the Tide and was the son of legendary Miami Dolphins coach Don Shula.

Speaking of Miami, what former Alabama quarterback, known by a three-letter name, became the starting quarterback of the Miami Dolphins in 2020? What is his full name?

Most people know him as Tua, but his name is Tuanigamanuolepola Tagovailoa. Tua came from Hawaii as a high school football phenom, and with seventeen offers to play on a college football scholarship, he decided upon Alabama and enrolled in 2017. His brother Taulia Tagovailoa played for the Tide before transferring to the University of Maryland. Both brothers are quarterbacks!

"The University can be many things for many people, but for the serious student it was and is the citadel and garden of mind."
—Dr. E. O. Wilson, BS, MS (Biology), 1950

How many times did the Crimson Tide play in the Rose Bowl? How many were losses? What was UA's biggest Rose Bowl victory? What year? Who did they play? What was the most recent?

Seven. One—the Tide won five out of six and tied one. The score at the UA's biggest Rose Bowl victory was 24–0 in 1931, playing Washington State. The most recent was the 2020 Rose Bowl against Notre Dame, with a Tide victory, 31–14.

How many UA students and alumni competed in the 2021 Summer Olympics in Tokyo? How many medals were won?

Four current students and seventeen alumni representing thirteen countries competed in Tokyo, and four medals were won: a gold medal for Remona Burchell in Women's Track and Field representing Jamaica; a bronze for Kirani James, in Men's Track and Field; a silver for Haylie McCleney representing the USA in Softball; and a silver for David Robertson, representing the USA in Baseball.

What former UA defensive player with a geographic nickname blocked the first two field goals of his career in a game against Tennessee?

"Mount Cody"—Terrence Cody, the award-winning defensive tackle in 2009. That game caught so much attention that he earned himself Heisman Trophy consideration, and was cited as being "the best player on what might be college football's top defense."

"The educational training and inspiration that I received at UA has opened numerous doors to educational opportunities that I perhaps otherwise would not have had. The discipline and desire for perfection required at UA has helped guide me through the arena of higher education and has proven to be of lasting value."
—Dr. Joffre Trumbull Whisenton, the first African American to receive a PhD from UA, 1968

What two Sugar Bowl records does the Crimson Tide hold?

It is the only team to have won three consecutive Sugar Bowls (1978, 1979, and 1980), and with eight victories, UA holds the Sugar Bowl record for most wins.

How many times has Alabama appeared in the Sugar Bowl?

Fifteen times! More than any other team in the game's history.

True or false: Alabama has more appearances in the Cotton, Orange, Rose, and Sugar Bowls than in all others combined?

That is indeed true! Roll Tide!

How did "The Crimson Tide" get its name?
It's purported to have been started by Hugh Roberts, a former sports editor of the *Birmingham Age-Herald.*

To what game was he referring to when he used that term?
An Alabama-Auburn game played in Birmingham in 1907 on a rain-soaked field and Alabama's valiant efforts to hold the heavily favored Auburn team to a 6–6 tie.

What sportswriter is credited for popularizing the name in the media?
Zipp Newman used the name often—he was a former sports editor of the *Birmingham News.*

What were popular nicknames before then?
"The Thin Red Line" and the "Crimson-White."

In what year did Alabama appear in its first bowl game?
1926. The first National Championship was that year, led by Wallace Wade. Alabama's victory against Washington was known as "the game that changed the South."

What year did Bama renew football relations with their in-state archrival Auburn University?
In 1948. They hadn't played each other for forty-one years.

Was the forty-one-year gap just in football?

No! The schools did not compete with each other in football, basketball, track, and baseball, with the exception of two postseason tournaments.

In what years were those two basketball tournaments?

1924 and 1941.

What 1935 Rose Bowl MVP went on to play professional baseball with the Cincinnati Reds?

Dixie Howell.

Who were the "Rocket 8"?

The 1955-56 men's basketball team! The Rocket 8 finished 21-3, 14-0 in the conference in 1955-56.

What 1950s UA basketball player held sixteen (of eighteen) UA individual records?

Jerry Harper.

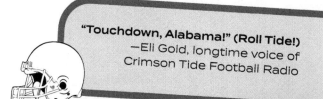

"Touchdown, Alabama!" (Roll Tide!)
—Eli Gold, longtime voice of Crimson Tide Football Radio

> "Perhaps its unique role in Alabama causes UA to have a special impact on students. It is more than just the process of educating, the imparting of skills, or the development of character and personality traits. It is a matter of the direction of one's vision; at least it was for me."
> —Robert Smith Vance, BS in Commerce from UA in 1950 and LLB degree from UA Law School in 1952

Who coached the "Rocket 8"?
Johnny Dee.

What UA grad has scored over fifteen thousand professional career points, and has been named to the NBA All-Star Team four times?
Latrell Sprewell (Class of 1992).

What two former UA students played against each other in the 1932 World Series, sharing the field with Babe Ruth and Lou Gehrig?
Joe Sewell, who played for the New York Yankees, and Riggs Stephenson of the Chicago Cubs.

Who won that World Series?
The Yankees!

What member of the 1933 football team was named for a Wild West performer, a man who was also his godfather?

B'Ho Kirkland—a lineman for the Tide. Kirkland played for the Crimson Tide from 1931 to 1933, and went on to play both professional football and professional baseball long before another Alabama "Bo" did the same.

What was the "Baby Tide"?

The UA freshman squad.

What UA coach, inducted into the Alabama Sports Hall of Fame in 2003, is the only inductee in a particular sport?

Coach Sarah Patterson. She served as the head coach of the Alabama Crimson Tide Women's Gymnastics team from 1979 to 2014. During her tenure, she built the program into one of the most successful in the history of college gymnastics.

What NBA player and UA alum had more NBA championships under his belt than any other active player?

Robert Horry (Class of 1992), with five NBA championships.

What NBA record did Horry break during the NBA Finals in 2005?

Most three-pointers made by any player in the NBA Finals, surpassing Michael Jordan's record of 42 three-point shots.

Who played Paul "Bear" Bryant in the 1984 film *The Bear*?

Gary Busey, who is probably best known for his portrayal of Buddy Holly in *The Buddy Holly Story* (1978).

Who was "The Dothan Antelope"?

Johnny Mack Brown.

Besides being a UA Rose Bowl MVP, what was Johnny Mack Brown known for?

A prolific star of westerns, he made movies in Hollywood, signing with MGM in 1926 and appearing in his last film in 1966.

Name two other "cowboys" that once played for the Crimson Tide.

Lee Roy Jordan went on to play for the Dallas Cowboys from 1963 to 1976, was their all-time tackle leader, and is in the Cowboys Ring of Honor. Dennis Homan played with the Cowboys from 1968 to 1970. And there are many, many more!

What annual reunion started in 1996, showing just how important Coach Bryant is to UA fans?

The annual Paul "Bear" Bryant Namesake Reunion, held at the Bryant Museum every fall since 1996. Conceived of by Paul Bryant Jr., more than six hundred namesakes have been recorded to date.

What was the last game that Coach Bryant coached? Who did Alabama play? What was the score of that game? Who was the MVP of that game?

The 1982 Liberty Bowl. Illinois. Alabama beat Illinois 21–15. Jeremiah Castille.

How many games did Coach Bryant win in his career?

A record 323 games.

How many times was Coach Bryant voted National Coach of the Year?

Three times. The award is now named in his honor!

What UA quarterback led Alabama to its first victory over the Fighting Irish?

Mike Shula. In a 1986 Kickoff Classic, Alabama defeated Notre Dame 28–10.

> "I remember many lessons Coach Bryant taught us, especially in his team talks. He talked about pride: pride in UA, pride in wearing the red jersey, and pride in ourselves. He taught us about dedication and the will to win. He showed us how discipline, especially self-discipline, would pay off in the end."
> —Steve Sloan, 1966 UA graduate and Tide quarterback

What distinction does the first captain of the Auburn football team have?

Frank Lupton, Auburn's first captain in 1892, was the first person to be born in the UA President's Mansion. He was the son of UA president Nathaniel Lupton.

What former UA basketball star stepped into the shoes of one of the most controversial college basketball coaches of all time? How did he stand out at Alabama?

Mike Davis, who replaced Bobby Knight at Indiana University in 2001. Davis was the first coach in Indiana history to begin his tenure with three straight 20-plus win seasons and three straight NCAA Tournament appearances and is Indiana's first African-American head coach. He played for the Tide from 1979 to 1983.

Give the surname of the family who had seven sons, five of whom made letters as pitchers for Crimson Tide baseball. What else were they known for?

Lary! The Lary Brothers—Joe, Al, Ed, Frank, and Gene—all pitched for the Tide, three of them going on to play professionally. The two other brothers were great pitchers too, but World War II prevented them from attending UA. They were also known for their fiddling prowess—all the Lary boys were also musicians. Al and Ed also played football at Alabama.

Name the one person who was a member of the coaching staff for nine modern-era national championships before his retirement.

Former athletic director Mal Moore, who was Coach Bryant's graduate assistant in 1964, Alabama's defensive backfield coach in 1965, and offensive coordinator for the 1973, 1978, 1979, and 1992 national championships as well as serving as AD for the first three national championships of the Saban era.

How did Mal Moore get his start with the Crimson Tide?

As a player—he completed his undergraduate degree from UA in 1963, a master's degree in 1964, and played football under Coach Bryant.

For what game did the Tide football team first wear crimson helmets? What color had they been previously? In what year did the team first start wearing hard football helmets?

The 1960 Astro-Bluebonnet Bowl against Texas. White with crimson stripes. 1930.

> "As a running back, you always want to be physical. Coming into Alabama from Florida, they all accepted me, they all loved me and all supported me."
> —Derrick Henry, UA alum and Heisman winner

What former UA student won a bronze medal in the 1972 Olympics in Munich?
Jan Johnson, in the pole vault.

How many national championships in Women's Gymnastics has UA won? In what years?
Six! 1988, 1991, 1996, 2002, 2011, and 2012. They have also won thirty-two NCAA Regional titles and ten Southeastern Conference Championships (2021, 2015, 2014, 2011, 2009, 2003, 2000, 1995, 1990, 1988).

Name four UA gymnasts who have been named SEC Athletes of the Year, an honor that spans all sports?
Four—Penny Hauschild in 1985, Dee Foster in 1990, Andree Pickens in 2002, and Jeana Rice in 2004.

Which two common household cleaning items are a quick way to make a statement on game day?
A box of Tide detergent and two rolls of toilet paper (roll, Tide, roll).

Under what coach did Paul "Bear" Bryant play football at Alabama?
Coach Frank Thomas.

Who is credited for bringing football to The University of Alabama? In what year?
W. G. Little of Livingston, Alabama. 1892.

"One of President Stuart Bell's expressed objectives is to increase the quality of our graduate students and programs. We are not Princeton, Yale, Harvard, University of Michigan, Berkeley, Carolina, or Virginia—this is the University of Alabama. Our goal was to showcase our intellectual work in the Department and in our University so that scholars coming here might be more inclined to send graduate students to our programs. I also wanted to provide networking opportunities in addition to our scholarship, cultural work and community outreach."
—Dr. Trudier Harris on the organization of the 2017 symposium "Black/White Intimacies: Reimagining History, the South, and the Western Hemisphere" at UA

What game brought Alabama football its first real national recognition? What was the score of that game?

The 1922 game where the Tide traveled to Philadelphia and defeated the powerful University of Pennsylvania team. Alabama beat Penn 9-7.

When was Alabama's first undefeated and untied football season?

The 1925 season was the first, under Coach Wallace Wade.

How many undefeated teams did Frank Thomas coach? Who was his college roommate?

Three—1934, 1936, and 1945. "The Gipper"—football legend George Gipp. They were roommates at Notre Dame.

What former UA assistant coach passed away just one hour before his induction into the Alabama Sports Hall of Fame? Under how many coaches did he serve at UA?

Hank Crisp. Five head coaches—he was at UA for thirty-six years, serving as AD twice during that tenure.

What remarkable piece of early Super Bowl history gives Alabama fans even more pride in the Tide?

The first three Super Bowl MVPs were former Alabama players. Bart Starr won it in January 1967 and 1968 for the 1966 and 1967 football seasons, and Joe Namath took the MVP in January 1969 for the 1968 season.

What building on campus was once known as the "Plaid Palace"? Why? Who is it named for? When was it built? What was it originally called?

Coleman Coliseum. In honor of former UA basketball coach Wimp Sanderson. Sanderson had a penchant for loud plaid sport coats. It was named for Jeff Coleman, a UA alum and administrator who never missed a UA bowl game. 1968. Memorial Coliseum.

Who has taken up the gauntlet with some killer plaid sport coats in recent years?

Alabama Men's Basketball coach, Nate Oats!

Have football seasons ever been canceled at Alabama?

Yes—in 1892, part of 1897 and 1898, when a faculty ruling prohibited games off-campus, and again in 1918 and 1943 because of World War I and World War II, respectively.

How did the UA team travel to the 1935 Rose Bowl?

In style—in a special train, which traveled across the country, leaving Tuscaloosa on December 21 for the January 5 game.

What was Alabama's overall record that year?

10-0.

"I shall remain grateful for the rest of my life for the contributions I received during the course of my time at UA. I have never adequately expressed my appreciation, and I remain indebted to all of those whose efforts enhanced and affected the rest of my life."
—Janie Ledlow Shores, a 1959 UA Law School graduate

How many shutouts did UA have that year? How many points did Alabama score that season? What was the crowning achievement for that season?

A remarkable eight shutouts, allowing only 13 points to be scored on them all season. They scored a whopping 217 points that season and crowned the season with a 24-0 victory at the Rose Bowl and being named national champions.

What former UA athlete won a medal in the 2004 Olympics in Athens?

Susan (Bartholomew) Williams won the bronze in the Triathlon.

What UA alum won four gold medals at two consecutive Olympics?

Swimmer Jon Olsen. He won in the 400m and 800m free relays in the 1996 games in Atlanta, where he was also the team captain, and in the 400m free relay and 400m medley relay in Barcelona—along with a bronze in the 800m free relay.

"We just gotta stop that ol' inside trap . . . sputtered around in the end zone. . . . We're just gonna play! We just gotta keep playin'."
—Interim head coach Joe Kines, in his epic 2006 Independence Bowl halftime interview

Who are the Crimson Cabaret?

UA's dance team—a favorite at Tide basketball games!

Name the UA athlete that took first place in an event at the Track and Field National Championship for the 2004–05 year?

Beth Mallory, who won first place in the discus, winning by a distance of more than seven feet. Her win marked the first UA event win since 1989.

What UA alum, competing for the Bahamas, won two medals in the 2000 Summer Olympics in Sydney?

Runner Pauline Davis took a gold in the 4x100 meter relay and a silver in the 200-meter dash.

Who was the first African-American men's scholarship basketball player at UA?

Wendell Thomas Hudson, who came to UA in 1970.

What UA alum won a gold in the 1984 Los Angeles Olympics and a silver in Seoul in 1988?

Runner Lillie Leatherwood, in the 4x400 meter relay.

What "venomous" quarterback led the Tide to an undefeated season in 1966?

Kenny "The Snake" Stabler. As a junior in 1966, he took over the starting quarterback position. He led the team to an undefeated, 11-0 season, which ended in a 34–7 rout of Nebraska in the Sugar Bowl. He went on to have a stellar NFL career, especially known for his decade with the Oakland Raiders.

What former UA basketball star made history as the first basketball Olympian at Alabama?
Antonio McDyess—he won a gold medal in the 2000 Olympics in Sydney.

Name the former UA baseball star who in that same year brought home a gold medal for baseball.
Tim Young.

What former UA head football coach was one of Coach Bryant's "Junction Boys"? What coaching victory did he have against his mentor?
Gene Stallings. As coach of Texas A&M, Stallings's team beat Alabama in the Cotton Bowl in 1967.

What NFL team did Gene Stallings coach?
The St. Louis Cardinals.

What member of the 1961 championship football team went on to coach at Tide archrival Tennessee?
Bill Battle.

Under what coach did Bama Baseball achieve six SEC championships?
Coach Tilden "Happy" Campbell had a lot to be happy about, achieving SEC championships in six of his first eight seasons at UA.

> "I do NOT read faster than other people. But one must be relentless. It is important to read every day. If you read 50 pages a day for six days, you have done a 300-page book. No magic there."
> —Don Noble, longtime professor emeritus of English, and the Emmy-nominated *Bookmark* host for thirty years on Alabama Public Television, on the subject of reading

In what years did UA's baseball team pitch a no-hitter?

In 2014, Justin Kamplain, Jay Shaw, and Geoffrey Bramblett combined to throw a nine-inning no-hitter for Alabama, beating Mississippi Valley State 7–0 in the second game of a three-game series. On March 31, 1993, Al Drumheller, John Collins, and Brett Sullenberger pitched a six-inning no-hitter at South Florida. The last nine-inning no-hitter before the 2014 game was on April 24, 1942, when Eddie Owcar did it against Mississippi.

What UA All-American football player and humanitarian became in 2002 the first African-American general manager in NFL history?

Ozzie Newsome Jr. for the Baltimore Ravens. He is currently their executive vice president of player personnel.

What remarkable distinctions does the Crimson Tide baseball team hold?

Many, but it should be noted that it leads the SEC in all-time wins with over 2,500 victories. The Crimson Tide have also had over sixty players make it to the major leagues, the most in the SEC.

What UA alum once held the major-league record for most consecutive baseball games played?

Joe Sewell! He played for 1,103 games straight. The record was bested by Lou Gehrig en route to his celebrated streak of 2,130 straight games.

What are the unofficial snack and drink of the Crimson Tide fan?

Golden Flake potato chips and Coca-Cola—they were the sponsors of *The Bear Bryant Show*, his Sunday postgame TV show.

> "I have met my best friends through this organization (Dance Alabama!), I'd say. It has a huge place in my heart because a lot of people get an opportunity to do something we love even if they don't want to do it in their profession. Whatever their situation they are able to audition and be a part of it."
> —An anonymous participant in the Dance Alabama! program

Name the father of a former UA player who served as the chaplain for UA athletes for many years.

The Reverend Sylvester Croom Sr. He later served as a Tuscaloosa pastor and community leader. His son Sylvester Croom played for the Tide in the 1970s, played in the NFL, and coached both college and pro football until his retirement.

Are there other elephant mascots in colleges and universities?

The University of Alabama is the only major university with an elephant as a mascot.

What year did the elephant become "Big Al"?

1979. Though the elephant was around for UA before that time, it was in the 1979 Sugar Bowl that the beloved mascot Big Al made his first appearance.

Who is "Big Al" named for?

Big Al was named for a local and very popular DJ, Al Brown, though many people think that it might be AL as in "Alabama," which is a pretty good guess!

Who was the first "Big Al"?

Melford Espey Jr., then a student, was the first to wear an elephant head costume to portray the Crimson Tide's unofficial mascot in the 1960s, before "Big Al" came to be. Espey had continued contact with the beloved mascot as a university administrator who was tasked by Bear Bryant to oversee the student group who wanted to establish Big Al as a mascot!

Does Big Al have a friend or a counterpart?

Yes! Big Al is sometimes joined by a female counterpart, an elephant named "Big Alice," at athletics events. Keep a lookout!

Other than Big Alice, can Big Al interact with other mascots?

Nope! It is a University rule because of a fight in 2002 that took place between Big Al and Seymour from Southern Miss. That incident has kept mascots apart in Bryant-Denny ever since.

In addition to "The Dothan Antelope" [Johnny Mack Brown], Alabama also had "The Alabama Antelope"—who was he? What National Championship did he have a part in?

Don Hutson, "The Alabama Antelope," was one of the best players in his era. He showcased elite speed, agility, and quickness, so his nickname was apt. Though not an Alabama native like Johnny Mack Brown, Hutson's Arkansas heritage didn't keep him from getting a nickname that included his adopted home state. Hutson starred for head coach Frank Thomas from 1932 to 1934 and helped lead an undefeated Alabama squad to a National Championship in 1934.